ALL THE BIBLE SAYS ABOUT TONGUES

ALL THE BIBLE SAYS ABOUT TONGUES

Bob Wells

ACCENT BOOKS
Denver, Colorado

 MEMBER OF
EVANGELICAL CHRISTIAN
PUBLISHERS ASSOCIATION

ACCENT BOOKS
A division of B/P Publications
12100 W. Sixth Avenue
P.O. Box 15337
Denver, Colorado 80215

Copyright © 1977 B/P Publications, Inc.
Printed in U.S.A.

All rights reserved. No portion of this book may be reproduced in any form without the written permission of the publishers, with the exception of brief excerpts in magazine reviews.

Library of Congress Number: 76-50298

ISBN 0916406-69-5

Contents

CHAPTER		PAGE
1.	Facing the Facts	6
2.	Tongues in the Gospels?	19
3.	When Tongues-Speaking Occurred	26
4.	Tongues at Corinth	36
5.	How Not to Speak in Tongues	46
6.	More on How Not to Speak in Tongues	56
7.	Some All-Important Guidelines	66
8.	Talk about Confusion!	77
9.	Practical Insights	90
10.	Tongues and the "Baptism"	99
11.	Be Filled with the Spirit	107
12.	Why We Must Take a Stand	117

/ALL THE BIBLE SAYS ABOUT TONGUES

Chapter 1

Facing the Facts

The charismatic movement is more than a movement. It may be described as an earthquake, for it has shaken personal lives, homes and churches. And proponents of the charismatic movement would quickly say "Amen" to the shaking. But many opponents of the movement would be just as quick to point out that an earthquake is a devastating thing, causing havoc and misery wherever it strikes. And, of course, others prefer to let their opinion rest somewhere between the two viewpoints.

Where does your opinion lie?

Some time ago I picked up a copy of *The Modern Tongues Movement* by the late Louis S. Bauman. I was shocked by the strong language employed by this former pastor, Bible expositor, and prophecy lecturer. He wasted no words in expressing his opinion of tongues-speaking, which is the chief emphasis of the charismatic movement. He charged: "In a day when so many, who solemnly profess to be children of God, are unconsciously becoming the victims of demon influences, no faithful shepherd can refuse to solemnly warn. Probably the most widely spread of all Satanic phenomena today is the demonic imitation of the apostolic gift of tongues. It is extremely common in the realms of spiritism, Mohammedism, and Mormonism. It is seen in witchcraft, in pagan oracles, in heathen temples and prophethoods, and all other neurotic manias and frenzies. It appeared very early in the history of the Christian church in that demonic movement known as Montanism. The first miracle that Satan ever wrought was to cause the serpent to speak in a tongue (Genesis 3:1). It would appear he is still working his original miracle."

Do Dr. Bauman's remarks shock you as they shocked me? If they do, let me suggest that you observe tongues-speaking in the critical light of Scripture, for I came to accept his remarks at face value after I had spent much research time in the Scriptures concerning the tongues controversy.

I realize that many who seem to be lovely, dedicated Christians will talk about their own personal experience with tongues and will urge others to become involved. They will make many extravagant and perhaps exciting claims as to what tongues-speaking has done for them and will do for you. Some of them will even go so far as to suggest that you may not even be saved if you do not speak with tongues.

Not Experience but Revelation

At the very outset of this book, I want to make it clear that I am not going to draw my conclusions from the experiences of men. I am going to concentrate on the clear, unmistakable teaching of the Word of God. Therefore, it is important to know everything the Bible has to say on the subject, and to consider those words carefully, for they are the most important words ever written on the subject!

A Few Things to Learn

With all the emphasis on the subject of speaking with tongues, one gets the impression that the Bible is filled with references to the subject. But the facts show the opposite. The subject of tongues receives only minimal treatment in God's Word. Out of sixty-six books in the Bible only three — Acts, Mark and I Corinthians — mention the subject. Only six of the 1,189 chapters in the Bible mention tongues. And only twenty-one of the Bible's 31,162 verses contain a reference to tongues.

Of further interest is the fact that the book of Acts makes only three references to the historical occurrence of "tongues." Mark's Gospel has a reference to tongues in the closing verses of chapter 16, but many scholars caution us against building doctrine on these verses, for they regard the passage as spurious, not being in the original manuscripts. In I Corinthians, tongues is simply listed as one of the spiritual gifts. Another reference tells us that tongues "shall vanish away."

Jesus did not use or refer to tongues. John the Baptist, who was filled with the Spirit, never spoke with tongues, nor did he mention them.

Tongues is not listed as part of the fruit of the Spirit. There are thirteen references in Acts to being filled with the Holy Spirit, and in only three instances is it stated that those who were filled with the Spirit spoke with tongues. In the other ten there is no reference to speaking in tongues. In no other place in the Bible where the fullness of the Spirit is mentioned is there any reference to tongues. And only one New Testament church was in any way involved in the use of tongues — the problem church of Corinth.

Scan the Passages

Let us now look quickly at the New Testament references to tongues.

Mark 16:17 is the first verse in the New Testament that mentions tongues, but, as I have said, it is considered by many Bible scholars to be spurious. We will discuss this verse in Chapter 2.

In Acts 2 we read the account of the outpouring of the Holy Spirit at Pentecost. This is the first of the three historical references of tongues recorded in Scripture. The tongues *(glossai)* used here were known languages. They were directed to unbelievers, from among the representatives of some seventeen nations, who were in Jerusalem at that time.

Acts 10:46 tells us of the second historical instance of speaking in tongues recorded in Scripture, happening eight years after Pentecost. Notice that according to verses 45,47 and Acts 11:15,17 what happened to these Gentiles was identical to what happened to the Jews on the day of Pentecost—they spoke with actual languages.

Five years later in the city of Ephesus men spoke in tongues. The story, recorded in Acts 19:6, outlines the third and last instance of a historical use of tongues.

In I Corinthians 12, tongues is mentioned three times. In verses 10 and 28 tongues is included in lists of spiritual gifts, and is given low status. In verse 30 we see that tongues-speaking is not for every Christian.

We see in I Corinthians 13:8 that the gift of tongues was temporary. Paul tells us here that tongues would automatically cease.

First Corinthians 14 has fourteen references to tongues, for it is the chapter in which Paul gives us guidelines and warnings about tongues.

This is the extent of what the New Testament says about tongues, and we will later study the passages in depth.

The Bible: Our Sole Authority

Please remember that the Word of God and what it teaches are under no circumstances established by what we experience. Rather, the validity of our experience must be determined by the clear teaching of the Word of God. The honest, conscientious Christian will accept nothing which is not clearly taught in the Word of God. The Holy Spirit speaks to us through the Bible, our sole authority for faith and practice. Everything that comes along under the guise of something new in religious trends and practices must be evaluated carefully in the light of the Word of God. So let's evaluate the subject of tongues in the light of Scripture.

Deception and Error

Part of the deception which characterizes the day in which we live is directed toward persuading people to develop an exaggerated opinion of charismatic doctrine. In huge conventions, meetings and rallies, through the use of the media, by means of books, pamphlets, and tracts, through the use of tapes and records, by careful organization, promotion and publicity, the charismatics create the impression that speaking in tongues is the ultimate experience of the Christian life! Listening to them, you get the impression that this unusual ecstatic experience is so super-important that it transcends all other considerations—without it, you just can't amount to anything at all for the Lord.

How Important Is Experience?

The charismatic theology is experience-oriented. Listening to them in person or on radio or TV you are made aware of the alleged importance of their many and varied experiences. They constantly talk of receiving "the baptism of the Holy Spirit" with its evidence, the gift of tongues. They speak of strange visitations, amazing visions, healing, miracles and emotional explosions.

But we need to realize that through their peculiar revelations, prophecies and visions they are adding to the Word of God. In their emphasis on experience, they ignore one of the major principles set forth in Scripture, for God's Word tells us that "we walk by faith, not by sight" (II Corinthians 5:7). Our only standard for faith and practice is the Word of God, not experience. Experience is never to be accepted as a substitute for the Word of God. In fact, it cannot even be *tolerated* when it in any way contradicts or clashes with the only authority to which we have any right to appeal.

"Don't Confuse Me with the Facts!"

With the charismatics, experience transcends doctrine. One experience is built upon another as evidence of the validity of their claims. When challenged to substantiate their claims with the Word of God, they appeal to their experience. The general attitude seems to be, "I don't care what the Bible says, I have had the experience. I have spoken in tongues!" In fact, this is the way one prominent speaker phrased it from the platform of a large charismatic convention.

Mormons, Mohammedans, Spiritualists and the adherents of many other non-Christian religions also say, "I have had the experience—I have spoken in tongues." But do we hear the charismatics defending these false religionists? They, too, have had an experience. It is comparable if not identical to the experience of the charismatics—but is it acceptable? The acceptability and legitimacy of an experience must not be judged by its popularity, its emotional impact and satisfaction, or the package in which it is presented, however attractive it may be. We must judge all of these experiences on the same basis—the Word of God.

Our evaluation of these experiences must not be based on the emotions or the warmth, friendliness and spirit of love which charismatics may give. Rather, it must be made on the basis of a careful comparison with Scripture's teaching. If the Bible teaches clearly and without any reservation that we are to speak with tongues, then no matter what, those of us who believe in the complete and final authority of the Word must speak with tongues.

Though an Angel Come from Heaven

But on the other hand, if Scripture does not teach us to speak in tongues, if the clear teaching of the Word indicates that we are *not* to speak in tongues, we must say, "Though an angel from Heaven preach contrary to God's own Word, we will have none of it."

I never cease to be amazed at the number of Bible-believing Christians who will excuse the errors of the charismatics by saying, "But they are so loving." Is their apparent love a significant factor in evaluating the experiences they propagate? The fact is, many of the most loving people I have ever met were members of unscriptural cults. Should I then suggest that because these cultists are so loving we must accredit their teachings and experiences? The same argument that pertains to them must be applied to the charismatics and all others.

The Holy Spirit Acts Sovereignly

Perhaps the best known charismatic is Oral Roberts. After making a good statement about the importance of the Word of God, he sets that statement aside and nullifies it altogether when he writes, "However, I wish to point out that sometimes the Holy Spirit acts sovereignly. We must learn that we must not allow ourselves to stereotype Him. At such times the spiritual ones know that it is God moving. On rare occasions, He will manifest a gift of tongues and interpretation, seemingly in a way that is not in accordance with the broad general rules laid down in the Scriptures. At the same time, He never contradicts Himself or does violence to His Word. The Holy Spirit is a perfect gentleman. We can trust Him" (from *The Baptism with the Holy Spirit*).

God's Word Is Never Superseded

What Oral Roberts is saying here is that sometimes the Holy Spirit acts contrary to the teaching of the Word, that He acts sovereignly in such matters. Following this unwarranted observation—which is without one scintilla of substantiation in the Word of God—he suggests that "we must not allow ourselves to stereotype" the Holy Spirit, after which he suggests in a subtle way, "At such times the spiritual ones know that it is God moving."

So, "spiritual ones" are to judge the activity of the Holy Spirit to determine whether or not God is moving. "Spiritual ones" will know. Since we are talking here about activities of the Holy Spirit apart from the guidelines of the Word of God, on what basis, then, are "spiritual ones" to make their judgment? The charismatics' answer, of course, is "experience."

But the answer is not valid. The fact is, Oral Roberts is wrong. His statement is entirely false, for it has no Biblical foundation. So-called "spiritual ones" have taken it upon themselves through the centuries to make such unfounded evaluations. The result can be seen in the tragic proliferation of cults and multiplied teachers spreading the doctrines of demons (I Timothy 4:1) around the world and bringing multitudes to destruction.

There is only one authority in this or any other matter—the Word of God. The Holy Spirit did not make any mistakes in writing His Word, not even in the sense of omissions which would have to be corrected by His "operating sovereignly"—ignoring the plain teaching of His Holy Book.

You owe it to yourself—to your personal spiritual knowledge and growth—to face the facts. Examine what the Bible has to teach about tongues. Do not be swayed by the testimonies of charismatics concerning their experiences. Yield to the authority of Scripture and make your decision on the basis of "Thus saith the Lord."

Chapter 2

Tongues in the Gospels?

*I*n my desire to learn what the Bible teaches about tongues, I began my study with the first book of the New Testament, the Gospel of Matthew. Carefully I searched Matthew's account of the life and ministry of our Saviour to see whether he made any mention of tongues. I did not find a word about speaking in tongues. So I went to the second Gospel—Mark—but found nothing there to indicate that God wants us to speak in tongues. My perusal of the Gospel of Luke met with the same results. Even John's Gospel, that says so much about abundant life, offered no mention of tongues.

I checked carefully the words of John the Baptist. Though he was filled with the Holy

Spirit from his mother's womb and spoke much about the ministry of the Holy Spirit, he uttered not one word about speaking in tongues!

I especially examined the words of Jesus, to whom the Holy Spirit was given without measure (John 3:34). Although He spoke much about the marvel, importance and power of the Holy Spirit's ministry, He said nothing about tongues!

Perhaps you are about to suggest that I have overlooked Mark 16:17: "They shall speak with new tongues." This verse is often referred to as containing the first mention of tongues in the New Testament. As a matter of fact, my study of this verse has led me to the conclusion that it should not be considered a part of the inspired original autographs of the New Testament.

Does It Belong?

C. I. Scofield comments: "The passage from [Mark 16] verse 9 to the end is not found in the two most ancient manuscripts, the Sinaitic and Vatican, and others have it with partial omissions and variations" *(The Scofield Reference Bible,* footnote following Mark 16).

H. B. Swete arrives at a similar conclusion in his *Gospel According to St. Mark,* where he points out that the addition of internal defects to that already mentioned distinguishes the passage from the rest of the book.

He concludes that it is impossible to resist these verses' belonging to a work of a different author.

Greek scholar A. T. Robertson comments, "When we turn to internal evidence the case against the passage is very much strengthened, proving conclusively that these verses could not have been written by Mark." He goes on to say that verses 8 and 9 don't fit together, and concludes that verses 9-20 were independently written.

Not Authentic, Not Authoritative

Since many outstanding New Testament scholars have challenged Mark 16:17 because of what they believe to be overwhelming evidence against its being a part of the original text, can we in good conscience consider it an authentic endorsement for the use of tongues?

In his commentary on Mark 16:17,18, Kenneth S. Wuest quotes A. T. Robertson as saying, "'The great doubt concerning the genuineness of these verses (fairly conclusive proof against them in my opinion) renders it unwise to take these verses as the foundation for doctrine or practice unless supported by other and genuine portions of the New Testament.'"

What Did Jesus Say?

Since there is not another word about

tongues in the Gospels, we must conclude that the four Gospels actually have nothing at all to say on the subject. This means that there is not a word about tongues from Matthew, Mark, Luke (in his Gospel) or John. Not even a word from John the Baptist! And is it not significant that even Jesus never used tongues or advocated their use?

In John 1:32-34, John the Baptist tells of seeing the Holy Spirit descending from Heaven like a dove and abiding on Jesus, but there is no mention of tongues. Throughout His entire ministry our Saviour taught His disciples about the Holy Spirit. He told them of the rivers of living water (John 7:38), of the Holy Spirit's indwelling the believer (John 14:17,18), and of the coming Comforter's ministry to believers (John 16:7-15). He breathed on the disciples and said, "Receive ye the Holy Ghost" (John 20:22) and told them of the Father's promise to give them power (Luke 24:49), but He never even hinted at tongues as something necessary or even profitable.

The Lord Jesus did many wonderful works while on earth. He healed multitudes, even to the point of restoring limbs and renewing life. He cast out demons and gave people a reason to live. He multiplied a sack lunch to feed thousands, and transformed a raging sea into a rippling lake, but He never spoke in or encouraged the use of tongues.

Christ founded and organized His body, the church, and gave His Spirit to her for power and boldness. He instructed us in the practical

Christian life and provided for our holy living, yet He didn't once mention tongues as being necessary or profitable.

The Saviour gave us a command to preach the gospel, make disciples and baptize them, and instruct them in His Word, but He did not include tongues as a part of His message. He taught us to pray, to study His Word, and to fellowship with others around His Table, but He did not instruct us to speak in tongues.

Our Lord promised to provide for all our needs, including eternal life, forgiveness, joy and peace. But He did not suggest that we have even the slightest need to speak in tongues.

Doesn't it seem odd that Christ "neglected" such an important area as tongues? He might have given us some idea about the purpose or use of the gift. But don't you agree that since He didn't mention tongues it suggests He never intended for us to get involved in tongues-speaking? Certainly our Lord isn't one to expect us to be proficient in an area we know nothing about. So the only logical conclusion I can reach is tongues-speaking is not something we should engage in. My attitude is firm: If the Lord Jesus Christ and His disciples didn't involve themselves in tongues, neither will I. I choose, rather, to invest my time in heeding those matters about which the Lord did give instruction. It seems to me that this is the best route to follow in order to please Him and build for eternity.

Chapter 3

When Tongues-Speaking Occurred

What is the Biblical record regarding the actual historical use of tongues? Dr. Luke, not only a physician, but also a fine historian, gives us the answer in the book of Acts. There are just three such instances in Scripture, all recorded in Acts. All other references to speaking in tongues are merely discussions about it—not historical records of occurrence.

Acts 2

The second chapter of Acts provides the first historical instance of speaking with tongues. In this chapter we have the central and, by all means, the most important message the Bible gives on the subject of tongues. It is actually the only detailed description of speaking in tongues given in the Scripture.

W. A. Criswell, pastor of the First Baptist Church of Dallas, Texas, summarizes the facts of this passage in his book, *The Holy Spirit in Today's World:* "In Jerusalem, on the day of Pentecost, the outpouring of the Holy Spirit was attended by three miracles: one, the sound of a rushing, mighty wind; two, the sight of a great flame of fire that, descending, divided into tongues which burned above the heads of the apostolic witnesses; three, the hearing on the part of men from the nations of the civilized world, each in his own tongue, the wondrous words of God. The gift of tongues at Pentecost was one in which the language spoken was understood by the different nationals. No interpreter was necessary. The languages spoken were not unknown tongues. They were the native languages of the hearing people."

Intelligible Languages

In Acts 2 there is no mention of an "unknown" tongue, nothing about a so-called "spiritual language," no "heavenly language." Granted, the languages used on the Day of Pentecost were foreign to those who were speaking, but at the same time they were known, spoken languages in the native countries of the hearers.

Evidence of the Filling by the Holy Spirit

Now, look at Acts 2:4, where we are told that when they were all filled with the Holy Ghost, they "began to speak." Please give careful consideration to those words, because they indicate the most important expression of the Holy Spirit's filling that we find in this chapter.

In Acts 1:8, Jesus had told the disciples that they would "receive power, after that the Holy Ghost is come upon you: and ye shall be witnesses unto me." He declared that the result and evidence of their receiving power through the Holy Spirit would be witnessing. Therefore, when we come to Acts 2:4 and read that they were filled with the Holy Spirit and His power, we should expect to find that evidence that Jesus spoke of. And we do—they "began to speak." In other words, they were indeed witnesses unto the Lord Jesus Christ, beginning in Jerusalem. The fact that they witnessed in other languages is not nearly so significant as the fact that they *did* witness. In fact, as we study the Word, we see that in every instance where men were filled with the Holy Spirit, the result and ever-present evidence of that fullness was effective witnessing for the glory of God.

When the people heard the message of the gospel in their own languages at Pentecost they were tremendously impressed. They could not understand how these unlearned men could speak in such a fashion. Because of their curiosity, and as a result of witnessing in various parts of the city ("when this was noised abroad"—verse 6), crowds gathered together. Then Peter, filled with the Holy Spirit, preached a magnificent message which resulted in great conviction and the conversion of a multitude. The record tells us in verse 41 that "they that gladly received his word were baptized: and the same day there were added unto them about three thousand souls." The purpose of Pentecost was to win souls to Christ and organize them into a New Testament church. This was wonderfully fulfilled. What a victory for the cause of the risen Christ!

Acts 10

The second instance of actual tongues-speaking is recorded in Acts 10, occurring eight years after Pentecost. God had sent Peter to Caesarea to preach the gospel in the Gentile household of Cornelius. By this God was showing the Jews that the gospel was for everyone, that He is no respecter of persons. His message of salvation is for all who will trust His Son as their Saviour, including the Gentiles.

The Gentiles who heard Peter's message that day were convicted by the Holy Spirit and accepted Christ as their Saviour. Even while Peter was still preaching, the Holy Spirit fell on them in great power and they began speaking in tongues. It would seem that the

Christians present at this gathering would rejoice in the salvation of souls and gift of the Holy Spirit. But they were too surprised to be thankful—imagine, Gentiles receiving the Holy Spirit! That was unheard of. God's people had always been the Jews, never the Gentiles. But there could be no mistake about it, God had manifested Himself to the Gentiles and had poured out His Spirit upon them. Peter testified to this fact when he inquired, "Can any man forbid water, that these should not be baptized, which have received the Holy Ghost as well as we?" (verse 47). Peter realized that God was beginning a new ministry to the Gentiles, and he informed his fellow believers of that fact by comparing this manifestation of the Holy Spirit to what had previously happened to them.

Even though God had revealed to Peter and those with him His intention to save the Gentiles and give them His Spirit, there were many Jewish Christians who were angry with Peter for going to the uncircumcised. They demanded an explanation for his behavior, so he recounted to them the whole story of God's calling him to Caesarea. He concluded his narrative with a final plea for them to understand and accept this new ministry of God. "Forasmuch then as God gave them the like gift as he did unto us, who believed on the Lord Jesus Christ; what was I, that I could withstand God?" (Acts 11:17). In effect, he was saying, "Who do you or I think we are that we can limit God to saving the souls of

Hebrews? If God wishes to pour out His Spirit on the Gentiles, I am not going to argue with Him."

Of special interest in this verse are the words "the like gift as he did unto us." Peter was indicating that the gift of the Holy Spirit given to the Gentiles was identical to what the Jews had received on the Day of Pentecost. How did he know this? Apparently the results were the same—they spoke with boldness, and they spoke in *intelligible human languages*—tongues. Had the Gentiles spoken in some unknown gibberish, Peter would have accused them of insanity, rather than defending their having received the Holy Spirit. But since he recognized their speech as a manifestation of the Holy Spirit, we must conclude that the tongues spoken in Acts 10 were, like those of Acts 2, known human languages.

Acts 19

The third historical instance of speaking in tongues took place in the city of Ephesus (Acts 19:1-7). Paul had come to Ephesus and there met twelve of John the Baptist's disciples. They had no doubt been baptized in John's name or by him, but they had not received Christian baptism—being immersed in the name of the Father, the Son, and the Holy Spirit. We know this because when Paul inquired as to their receiving the Holy Spirit, they replied that they had never even heard of the Holy Spirit. Paul proceeded to instruct them in the matter of Christian baptism, and baptized them in the name of Christ. Then he laid his hands on them and "the Holy Ghost came upon them; and they spake with tongues, and prophesied" (verse 6).

This is all the narrative says about their speaking in tongues—the fact that indeed they did so. Since it says nothing else about the incident—the nature or endurance of the tongues—we have to make some assumptions. First of all, notice that there is no mention of an interpreter. Therefore, the men present must have understood what was said, thus eliminating the possibility of some form of "heavenly language" or ecstatic gibberish. We may also assume that since this tongues-speaking followed the filling with the Holy Spirit, it was identical to those instances recorded in Acts 2 and 10. Therefore, we can conclude that the tongues used here were intelligible, spoken languages, and not some unknown gibberish.

Finally, we need to take a close look at the endurance of these tongues used in Ephesus. Was this gift something that continued for years, or was it a one-time occurrence? The Scripture does not come right out and say one way or the other, but we can get a good idea from the book of Ephesians. In this epistle, Paul gives extensive teaching on the ministry of the Holy Spirit. He tells us that we are sealed with the Spirit, and that as believers we are "builded together for an habitation of God through the Spirit" (Ephesians 1:13; 2:22; 4:30). He further informs us of his prayer that we be strengthened by the Holy

Spirit (3:16). We have the instruction to "be filled with the Spirit" (5:18), and are warned not to grieve Him (4:30). Paul also tells us to pray in the Spirit (6:18), but nowhere in this epistle does he instruct us to speak in tongues, through the Spirit or otherwise. In fact, he doesn't even make reference to tongues at all, even though the Ephesians had spoken in tongues.

Surely if tongues were as important as many today try to tell us, Paul would have said something about them to this Ephesian church. And certainly if the church had continued using tongues, Paul would have commended them or given them further instruction in the matter. But apparently tongues was not intended to be permanent.

The Ephesian church was well-informed as to the ministry of the Holy Spirit, but they were not given any instruction pertaining to the use of tongues. We must therefore conclude that tongues-speaking was a temporary gift given for a special purpose—witnessing—and that it is not necessary today in a Spirit-filled life.

Chapter 4

Tongues at Corinth

*N*ow we come to the consideration of Paul's first letter to the church at Corinth. This was a church full of division and disobedience, of carnality and puffed-up pride. Because of this puffed-up pride, they tolerated immorality that was not even mentioned among the pagans; they went to law against one another; they got drunk at the Lord's Table. And they spoke with tongues!

Is it not significant that out of all the New Testament epistles, this is the only one in which reference to tongues is made? Eliminating the disputed verse in Mark, tongues is not referred to in the Gospels; nor is it mentioned in Revelation—only in Acts and in this first letter from Paul to the carnal Corinthian church!

Real Languages

Paul Van Gorder, in his book *Charismatic Confusion*, gives some interesting insights to the substance of the tongues referred to in I Corinthians. He points out that this epistle was written about six years before the book of Acts, and argues that when Luke wrote Acts he was aware of Paul's earlier use of the same term, "tongues." It is doubtful that Luke would choose this word to mean languages if Paul had used it to mean non-intelligible gibberish. So it seems only logical to conclude that the word "tongues" in I Corinthians refers to actual, spoken languages.

Greek scholar Spiros Zodhiates gives us some further proof that Paul meant actual languages when he referred to tongues. He points out that "there are two Greek words used to express 'speaking'—'lalein' and 'legein.' The first means articulated words (speech) as contrasted with silence, without reference to thought content. The second word for 'speaking' is 'legein,' 'to say, to discourse.' Legein, saying, is offering thought in an orderly way; but lalein, speaking, is the articulation of words as they come to you.

"It is always the word 'lalein' that is used in the expression 'speaking with tongues.' Why is this? In the three historical instances of speaking with tongues recorded in the Acts, . . . God is concerned about conveying His divine message to man. The Holy Spirit acts upon the believer to speak, not the product of his own mind, but the message of

God. The believer is merely the agent of transmission. He could not, through his own thought processes, put together words of a language that he did not understand and make sense to his hearers. Yet it is evident that the hearers of those who were enabled supernaturally to speak with tongues understood what was being said in all these historic instances. It was the Holy Spirit who gave the words and put them together so that they were intelligible to the hearers and conveyed the thoughts of God, not those of the speaker."

Zodhiates comments further: "Very interestingly, the word 'lalein' is rarely used in modern Greek. For the most part, the Greeks prefer the word 'legein' when referring to speech, perhaps to emphasize their feeling that when we speak we had better have something to say! This, in fact, is what Paul is saying to the Corinthians. He calls their unintelligible vocalizing 'lalein glucise,' which indicates that they were uttering sounds devoid of thought. Such sounds had to be interpreted, if such a thing were possible. This is what the apostle condemns in I Corinthians 14."

Tongues in I Corinthians 12

There are just four references to tongues in I Corinthians 12. The first two are in verse 10—"divers kinds of tongues" and "the interpretation of tongues." The third is in verse 28, where we read "diversities of tongues." In each case tongues is included in a list of spiritual gifts.

There are in Scripture two other lists of spiritual gifts—Romans 12:6-8 and Ephesians 4:11—but in these lists tongues is not mentioned at all.

As we read through these four lists of gifts, we find mention of nineteen distinct gifts. Does it not seem strange that our charismatic friends seem to be primarily preoccupied with two of them (tongues and healing), especially with tongues? Obviously, to have the ability to heal men supernaturally as did Jesus and the apostles (which, if fully realized, would mean that hospitals could be emptied and the sick healed en masse) would provide an experience that would be very exciting in the flesh. And apparently there is some kind of a satisfying, ecstatic, emotional experience related to speaking in tongues. But why is it that such gifts as wisdom, knowledge, faith, teaching, prophecy, helps, giving, and showing mercy rarely receive even the slightest consideration? Why is tongues such a popular item among charismatics? Doesn't this seem odd, since the Scriptures do not promote tongues-speaking?

Do All Speak in Tongues?

The fourth reference to tongues in I Corinthians 12 is in verse 30 where Paul asks, "Do all speak with tongues?" This is a rhetorical question by which Paul is telling us that not everyone should have the gift of languages. It is important to keep this in mind in view of the fact that many of the charismatics insist that the one universal evidence of the fullness of the Holy Spirit is speaking in tongues.

Prediction: Tongues Will Pass Away

Examining the thirteenth chapter of I Corinthians we are confronted with an interesting statement with reference to tongues. W. A. Criswell clearly explains this passage in his book, *The Holy Spirit in Today's World:*

"When Paul comes to speak of tongues in I Corinthians 13:8, he not only changes the verb but he also changes the voice of the verb he uses. As with 'prophecies' and as with 'knowledge' we would have expected him to use the future passive *katargethesontai*. Not so, He uses a different verb, *pauo*, 'to cause to cease,' and he changes the voice from passive to middle, *pausontai*, which literally translated means, 'tongues shall make themselves to cease,' or 'tongues shall automatically cease of themselves.'

"Most emphatically Paul avows that 'tongues will automatically cease of themselves.' In the next verse, I Corinthians 13:9, they have already ceased in his thinking, for he mentions the gift of prophecy and he names the gift of knowledge but he pointedly omits the gift of tongues. Tongues are needed no longer."

Dr. Criswell continues by pointing out that

in the other epistles Paul wrote, he did not refer to speaking in tongues. The reason for this is the fact that tongues was the first of the sign gifts to cease. It ceased almost immediately. It was a gift belonging only to the infant church. When the church began to mature, it no longer needed this sign, just as a grown man no longer needs his rattle or teething ring, for they are implements of his childhood.

A Worthy Example?

The church that spoke with tongues—was it a spiritual church, dominated and directed by the Holy Spirit? Was it obvious to others that the Holy Spirit ruled in their midst, controlling their ministry, their speech, their conduct and their relationships? This is not what we would expect from the church that spoke with tongues if tongues is indeed the evidence of the Holy Spirit's control!

But check the record a little more carefully. See for yourself what the Word has to say. One of the chief characteristics of this church was division: "I beseech you, . . . that there be no divisions among you" (I Corinthians 1:10); "For ye are yet carnal: for whereas there is among you envying, and strife, and divisions" (I Corinthians 3:3); "when ye come together in the church, I hear that there be divisions among you" (I Corinthians 11:18). Certainly the tongues-speaking wasn't making the slightest contribution to the spirituality of the Corinthian church. Why, then, do charismatics assume it will help our twentieth-century churches?

We learn from Paul's letter to the Corinthians that there were contentions in the church (I Corinthians 1:11). The word *contention* means "wrangling" or "quarreling." Their differences of opinion had degenerated into factional quarrels. The church was broken up into coteries and parties, and all the members chose up sides. "Now this I say, that every one of you saith, I am of Paul; and I of Apollos; and I of Cephas; and I of Christ" (verse 12); "For while one saith, I am of Paul; and another I am of Apollos; are ye not carnal?" (I Corinthians 3:4). Some liked the orator, some the teacher, others liked the exhorter. Some liked plain preaching and some liked fancy phrases. Others, who were just a little bit "holier than thou" said, "We'll just follow Jesus."

Talk about a divided, obstinate group of Christians. It is impossible to conclude that they were knowledgeable about the Spirit's ministry.

Paul tells us that the Corinthians were carnal (fleshly), for they acted like children. He calls them babies and reports that they had to be fed with milk instead of with meat, which is reserved for the mature person. Instead of acting like Spirit-controlled persons, they were acting like the "natural man," who doesn't know the things of the Spirit of God because he has never been saved (I Corinthians 2:14—3:4)! Paul rebuked them, "I, brethren, could not speak unto you as spiritual."

Added to all these shortcomings and deficiencies, the Corinthians were "puffed up for one against another" (I Corinthians 4:6). Paul charged, "Some are puffed up as though I would not come to you" (verse 18). They were even puffed up over their immorality (I Corinthians 5:2)! Paul was quick to tell them, "I write not these things to shame you, but as my beloved sons I warn you" (I Corinthians 4:14). But even though Paul called them "beloved sons," they were not what you could call a spiritual group.

If we were to select a church which professes to be Bible-believing and Spirit-controlled, describe such a church in the same terms with which Paul described the church at Corinth, and offer that church as an example of the fullness of the Holy Spirit, we would be laughed out of the country! And yet, the church at Corinth is supposed to have been the Holy Spirit-filled church with the "evidence" of speaking in tongues, according to charismatics. Doesn't it seem a little difficult to accept that? Isn't it obvious that there is a good deal wrong with such a belief? This becomes even more certain as we look carefully at I Corinthians 14.

Chapter 5

How Not to Speak in Tongues

*W*e come now to the final chapter in the Bible dealing with this subject of tongues—I Corinthians 14—written by the Apostle Paul under the direction of the Holy Spirit. It was for the specific purpose of dealing with the problems which had developed in the Corinthian church over the use of tongues. I think a fair and objective analysis of the chapter forces us to conclude that Paul is telling us that the Corinthian use of tongues was not what God had intended.

Because this is a controversial chapter and the only chapter that gives any kind of instructions, guidelines or restrictions for the use of tongues, we will examine it with great care. It begins with a general, yet extremely important statement. Paul instructs the Christians at Corinth to "Follow after [pursue] . . . and desire spiritual gifts." (The word "gifts" is not in the original but is understood from the context and thus was supplied by the translators.) Paul then instructs the Corinthians to desire "rather [moreover] that ye may prophesy."

At this point a word of explanation concerning the word "prophecy" is in order. In his book *I Once Spoke in Tongues* Wayne A. Robinson, a disillusioned former charismatic, tells us that those who believe prophecy refers only to predicting the future are mistaken. The first-century meaning of the word "prophecy" was simply forthtelling, much as a preacher does today. Paul used the word "prophecy" to mean the declaration of the divine revelation, the inspired proclamation of eternal truth.

Prophecy is in a language that others understand. Its object is neither self nor God, but others to whom God wants to speak, using us as His instruments. On the other hand, we see that in verse 2 Paul declares that "he that speaketh in an unknown tongue speaketh not unto men, but unto God: for no man understandeth him, howbeit in the spirit he speaketh mysteries."

Look Again

To gain a greater understanding of this chapter, we need to realize two things. First of all, the word "unknown" does not occur here or anywhere else in this chapter in the original language. It was supplied by the translators to express their understanding of the Corinthian phenomenon—that it was a language unknown among men, not human, not understandable; a fabricated language that was not really a language at all.

Next, notice the word "spirit." It does not refer to the Holy Spirit, but rather to the spirit of the one speaking in a tongue. We see this word again in verse 14, where it is used in conjunction with the word "my." Not only does the grammatical structure prove that this is man's spirit, but the very nature of the Godhead tells us that the Holy Spirit would not speak unintelligible words. Again we see in verses 15,16 the word "spirit." Here, too, it means man's spirit. The Holy Spirit does not appear anywhere in this 14th chapter. I conclude, then, that the Corinthian utterances were merely the creation of their own spirits.

Speaking to God

Referring again to verse 2, we see that "he that speaketh in an unknown tongue speaketh not unto men, but unto God." Here Paul indicates that the Corinthians practiced the use of a language that was *unknown*—not understandable. Apparently it was just a loud emotional outburst of sounds. But just because Paul recognizes the practice among the Corinthians does not mean that he approves of it.

He goes on to say that they speak with such strange sounds that they are obviously not speaking to men. So the only conclusion that he can come to is that they are speaking to God. Notice that he did not indicate that the sounds are ordained of God or even that they ever reach God's ears, but merely that God is evidently the intended hearer.

Paul then carefully sets forth his criticisms of this practice. "I have concluded that since this language you use isn't understandable to men, it must be directed to God. But why would anyone want to talk with God—especially in public worship—in a language that doesn't make sense to anybody else?" This is the gist of Paul's criticism.

It is true that God understands *all* languages, but when *we* don't know what we are saying, we cannot pray intelligently, nor can others enter in with us in prayer.

Prophecy the Better Choice

In verse 3 we see that "he that prophesieth speaketh unto men edification, and exhortation, and comfort." What a contrast to the senseless babble of verse 2! This "prophecy" had three distinct purposes: first, *edification*, meaning "building up." It is set forth in contrast to the fleshly selfishness of speaking in a babble that does not make sense and which could not possibly build up anyone (verse 4). Secondly, *exhortation*, or encouragement, which also must be understood to be profitable. Thirdly, *consolation* or comfort. This Greek noun, which appears nowhere else in the New Testament, has special reference to the comfort Christians need because of hostile opposition. And we will receive this comfort from clear, understandable preaching.

Use Those Languages

As we come to verse 5 we find a passage that is not only badly misunderstood but is also frequently misquoted: "I would that ye all spake with tongues." If you have been following carefully along in your Bible, you may have noticed that the translators did not render this as "unknown tongues" as they did in verse 2 and other places in this chapter. They knew Paul would not have desired that the Corinthians use a senseless babble, so they translated the word as "tongues," meaning *understandable human languages.* Paul is simply saying that he favors using other languages, in addition to your own, *for preaching the gospel.* Without a doubt Paul remembered that God had given real languages to the apostles in Acts for the preaching of the gospel. He is not contrasting speaking in foreign languages with prophesying (preaching or witnessing), but suggests that one makes the other more fully possible. Prophesying makes the knowledge of languages useful for God's glory, and knowing foreign languages makes the spread of the gospel easier and more effective.

Paul commends speaking in various languages, but he insists that they must be languages that others understand. He says that if you want to use other languages, make sure you have an interpreter so that others in the church may be edified. If God has not provided an interpreter, it is better just to preach in your own language (verse 5), Paul tells the Corinthians.

Seek to Edify

Please notice that the Holy Spirit caused Paul to emphasize this matter of *edification*—building up the local church. The word is used, in one form or another, seven times in this chapter. First, in verse 3 it is given as one of the purposes of prophesying. In verse 4 it is used twice: to indicate the selfishness of the one speaking in tongues and in contrast, to show the unselfishness of those who prophesy. In verse 5, it is used in the statement "greater is he that prophesieth than he that speaketh with tongues, except he interpret, that the church may receive edifying." In verse 12 we are told to "seek that ye may excel to the edifying of the church." In verse 17 it is revealed that the unlearned are not edified or built up through tongues-speaking. Finally, in verse 26 we are told to "let all things be done unto edifying."

In verses 6-12 Paul is saying that tongues-speaking does not bring about the edification of the church that is so imperative to an effective ministry. He says in effect, "Dear friends, suppose I should speak to you in a language you don't understand—would that help you? No, of course not. But on the other hand, if I speak clearly what God has revealed, if I share the things I know, if I tell what will happen, and if I explain the great truths of God's Word—that is exactly what will help you, for it is what you need.

"Consider musical instruments—the flute, or the harp. They illustrate the need for speaking in plain, simple languages. No one will recognize the music the flute is playing unless each note is formed clearly. And if the bugler doesn't sound the right call, how will the soldiers properly respond? So it is, if you speak to a person in a language he doesn't understand, how will he know what you mean? If someone speaks to me in a language I do not know, we remain strangers. His words are useless to me, for I get nothing out of them. So it is with your babbling—it is useless to others.

"Since you so anxiously desire the gifts of the Spirit, ask Him for the best gifts—the ones that will build up the whole church, rather than those that only benefit the user. Ask that you may preach the Word, so that your words will result in the edification of other believers."

Pray That You May Interpret

Now, on the basis of the preceding

instruction concerning the importance of the edification of the church, Paul proceeds in verse 13 to instruct the church at Corinth to "let him that speaketh in an unknown tongue pray that he may interpret." He does not forbid speaking in tongues in the church, but merely admonishes those who wish to do so to ask for the gift of interpretation that they may inform the listeners of what they are saying.

Paul gives this instruction because he is much concerned about the "unlearned" layman who may be a new Christian and therefore is limited in an understanding of the things of the Lord. How in the world can an uninformed person possibly say "Amen" to utterances that don't make sense? The ecstatic emotional babble used by the Corinthians needed to be interpreted in order to fulfill the purpose of spiritual gifts—edification of fellow believers.

Chapter 6

More on How Not to Speak in Tongues

More on How Not to Speak in Tongues/ 57

"*I* thank my God, I speak with tongues more than ye all.*"* As we look at these words from I Corinthians 14:18, we know that Paul wrote them, but do we know what they mean? This is another of the passages which is so often misunderstood and misinterpreted. Did Paul really have the gift of tongues? The answer is clear when you examine the passage carefully.

Paul Did Not Have the Gift of Tongues

Some of our friends in the charismatic movement say that Paul had the "gift of tongues." But as John R. Rice says in his book, *The Power of Pentecost*, "Now if Paul ever had a gift of tongues, the Bible does not mention it. When Paul was filled with the

Holy Spirit first, in Acts 9:17, no mention is made of the gift of tongues. Paul wrote fourteen of the 27 books in the New Testament, over half of the whole New Testament (if we include Hebrews, as I believe we must). We know more about Paul from the Bible than about any other Bible character except possibly David. And we have far more of his own words about himself than from any other man mentioned in the whole Word of God. And there is never a mention of Paul speaking miraculously by a gift of tongues. Without any word in the Bible to the contrary we believe Paul must refer [in I Corinthians 14:18] to the language, Koine Greek, in which Paul wrote his epistles and preached, though it was a foreign language, not his native Aramaic."

Regarding this 18th verse Spiros Zodhiates says, "To many, Paul's declaration that he spoke with tongues more than the Corinthians did is a real puzzle. Up to this point, and again later in the chapter, he condemns the Corinthians who spoke in a mysterious manner. Why does he here thank God that he does the very thing that he condemns? The only logical conclusion, is that Paul is talking about two different ways of speaking with tongues. When Paul mentions the Corinthian practice of speaking with tongues, he means unintelligible utterances not reducible to language forms, originating in the Corinthians' own spirits and emotions. When Paul refers to this, he usually used the singular form, 'speaking in a tongue.' In the Greek text, the word 'tongue' in its metaphorical meaning, referring to speech and not the physical organ, takes the singular form in verses two, four, thirteen, fourteen, nineteen, twenty-six, and twenty-seven. This is justifiably identified in the King James Version as 'an unknown tongue,' despite the fact the word 'unknown' does not occur in the Greek text. It is unknown to linguists; it is not spoken by any linguistic group of people; it cannot be reduced to phonetic syllables.

"When Paul speaks of his own ability to speak with tongues, he does not mean unintelligible utterances but known languages employed for the purpose of making the grace of God known to men. We must conclude that whenever known intelligible languages are meant, Paul uses the plural form, 'tongues,' and not 'a tongue' (see verses 5,6,18,21, and 23). Thus, in verse eighteen, which we are now examining, we find Paul saying, 'I thank my God, I speak with tongues more than ye all.' By this he means known intelligible languages, native to various groups of people who can understand them without the use of an interpreter."

Understanding Is the Key

In verse 19 Paul claims that "in the church [an assembly of believers and any others who might be present], I had rather speak five words with my understanding [utilizing my reasoning powers], ... than ten thousand words in an unknown tongue." By this Paul suggests that if he were to use some foreign language that the people cannot understand, or speak in some babble, he would not be using his right mind.

At all times, Paul was concerned primarily about his audience and about his accountability to God in the matter of ministering unto edification. His purpose was to "teach" or "instruct by word of mouth." In the use of the word "others" in this verse, Paul suggests that his primary concern should not be for himself, but for the other believers in the congregation. Realizing that speaking in an unintelligible babble would benefit no one except himself, he says he would rather speak something he and others understand, so by his speech he could edify others.

Sign for the Jews

We see in verse 22 that the supernatural gift of languages was for a specific purpose. It was for a sign! But apparently the Corinthian believers of Paul's day were like so many of their followers today—lacking in Scriptural understanding of the real purpose of the gift of tongues and thus needing Paul's instruction in the matter.

It is clearly taught in the Scriptures that signs are for the Jews (I Corinthians 1:22). This is evidenced by the fact that the Jewish leaders came to Jesus during His earthly ministry saying, "Master, we would see a sign from thee. But he answered and said unto them, An evil and adulterous generation seeketh after a sign" (Matthew 12:38,39). On another occasion they asked, "What sign shewest thou then, that we may see, and believe thee?" (John 6:30). In I Corinthians 14:21, Paul refers to a prophecy in Isaiah 28:11,12 to tell us that the main reason God caused some of His people to speak in foreign languages was for a special witness—a sign—to unbelieving Jews. This prophecy was fulfilled on the day of Pentecost, when the Lord caused those who had gathered together in the upper room to supernaturally speak with other languages to those Jews from "every nation under heaven" who were in Jerusalem at the time.

Not for Believers

In I Corinthians 14:22 the specific purpose of the gift of tongues is stated. It is a "sign . . . to them that believe not"; and conversely, it is "not to them that believe." In other words, tongues is of no value and has no application whatever for the believer. Those who have trusted in Christ do not need any outward sign or miracle such as took place at Pentecost. They have the testimony of Scripture.

By way of contrast, Paul tells us that "prophesying serveth not for them that believe not, but for them which believe." The word "prophesying" means "teaching or declaring God's Word," or simply performing the regular ministry of proclaiming the gospel. Believers need to be instructed and edified concerning the Word of God and the things of the Lord, and intelligent, understandable proclamation of the truth is the means for such instruction and edification.

Prophecy Superior

In verses 23-25 we see that what the Holy Spirit desires for the unbeliever can be accomplished through the preaching of the Word of God. The use of tongues for people who cannot understand their message does not make sense. It is the preaching of the Word of God which produces conviction and results in the experience Paul describes—"and so falling down on his face, he will worship God, and report that God is in you of a truth" (verse 25).

"Unto Edifying"

When Paul asks in verse 26, "How is it then, brethren?" he is asking in effect, "What, then, is the result of our discussion to this point?" In the preceding verses he had been talking about the superiority of the gift of prophecy and the extreme importance of properly communicating the truth, and had insisted that they minister in a manner that can be readily understood. But the key to understanding what Paul had in mind in verse 26 is the emphasis on the words, "Let all things be done unto edifying." Paul is saying that when you come together there will be some who would have psalms, some might teach, others might have a special revelation (disclosing or unveiling anything hidden). Singing of psalms, teaching, revealing—all require the use of speech. Naturally the words must be expressed intelligibly in order to edify others in the church.

But we see also that there may be someone in the church who "hath a tongue." We have learned that the singular form, "tongue," refers to ecstatic babble as practiced by the Corinthians, and so it is here. Paul is not as concerned about the first three manifestations of worship as he is about the speaking in an unknown babble and the interpretation of such speaking. It is to these that Paul's command applies: "Let all things be done unto edifying." Singing, teaching, and revelation already meet this requirement; but babbling without thought or any consideration for those who listen falls short of the goal.

The Proper Manner

Paul instructs tongues-speakers to make sure their babbling has interpretation. The word "interpretation" comes from a word from which we get our English word "hermeneutics," which is the science of interpretation or explanation, and means *to make clear with words, to explain, to expound.* Paul says emphatically, "No one is to speak in an unknown tongue unless there is an interpreter present," because when the hearer cannot understand, he can receive no possible benefit. So *interpretation is necessary*.

In no other way could speaking in tongues be tolerated, and even when interpreted it is to be only to fellow believers, not to unbelievers. Unbelievers would reason that anyone who could speak so as to make sense and yet would choose to do otherwise was not in his right mind. That's why Paul tells the Corinthians, in the spirit of loving tolerance, that if they insist on this practice of ecstatic utterances, they must limit their practice to the circle of believers, and then only if an interpreter is present. Paul does not recommend the practice, but he realizes that the believer hearing an interpretation of such sounds without sense might find some uplift in it. Therefore he tolerates it in favor of speaking in an uninterpreted babble before unbelievers.

Paul realized that since speaking in tongues originated in man's own spirit, the interpretation was an equally human fabrication. But he accepted things as they were. In love he suggests, "If you feel you are saying something when you make these sounds, let someone interpret, so that others may benefit if possible." Paul was not as much concerned about eradicating this practice as he was in establishing guidelines that would ultimately cause the Corinthians to abandon any practices that involved disregard for others.

More on How Not to Speak in Tongues/ 65

Chapter 7

Some All-Important Guidelines

The carnal church of Corinth was characterized by excesses and disorders. For example, of all the churches on record, theirs is the only one where the members got drunk at the Lord's Table. Strict guidelines had to be laid out for them in order to correct the problem. And now, Paul must deal with the serious tongues problem. It, too, had gotten out of hand and there must be restrictions and guidelines imposed to limit the excesses and set up some sort of an orderly process. These restrictions and guidelines are detailed for us in the remaining verses of I Corinthians 14, beginning with verse 27.

Paul begins by telling the Corinthians that if someone is going to speak in tongues, here is how it should be done. "Let it be by two, or at the most by three, and that by course; and let one interpret." This limits the number of people who can speak in an ecstatic, unintelligible language at any one service. "That by course" means "in turn," obviously precluding the possibility of more than one speaking at a time.

Only What Is Understood Can Edify

Paul's third requirement—"let one interpret"—brings him a step closer to helping the Corinthians realize the futility of the whole business of tongues (babble) and its interpretation. It is obvious that only what is understood can edify, yet when the Corinthians spoke in a strange tongue, often no one was able to interpret. "If there be no interpreter," Paul says in verse 28, "let him keep silence in the church; and let him speak to himself, and to God." Perhaps this is a polite way of saying, "Since you cannot be sure in advance that what you will say in an unknown tongue can be interpreted by someone, don't perform this exercise in public at all. Don't be involved in having said something before the assembly that cannot be understood or that does not make sense. Unless you can make yourselves readily understood in church, it is better to keep quiet."

"The Power of the Holy Ghost"

There is no record of God ever having spoken in a language understood by no one. Why, then, should He cause His children to do so? We are driven back again to the conclusion that both the speaking and the interpretation were expressions of man's emotional nature and came from his own spirit.

But the charismatics claim that just the opposite is true. Oral Roberts, a prominent charismatic leader, says, "We know further that one can speak in tongues only through the power of the Holy Ghost. . . . The believer exercising a gift of tongues is really possessed of God at that time. The gift and the believer seem to become one. Together, the believer and the gift become God's instrument to meet certain needs of the people." In other words, he is saying that when a person speaks in tongues he is speaking in the power of and under the control of the Holy Spirit. I think that in this, Oral Roberts fairly represents the position of the charismatics.

The Holy Spirit Cannot Violate His Word

Because of the voluminous testimony given by those who have attended charismatic meetings and from the frank admissions of charismatic leaders and writers, we know that the guidelines set forth in the Bible regarding speaking in tongues are frequently violated. Sometimes there have been outbursts of tongues in the midst of a meeting, contrary to the spirit and purpose of the meeting, and without interpretation. Frequently several have spoken in tongues simultaneously. And many times there have been more than three such messages in a given meeting.

These violations of the specific instructions of the Word of God (inspired by the Holy Spirit) present us with a serious dilemma. Can we assume that the Holy Spirit deliberately violates His written Word? The Holy Spirit is God, and as such He is absolutely perfect in every way. We have to acknowledge not only that He *would not* contradict His Word but that He *could not* do so by virtue of the attributes of His deity.

The Scripture Alone

Why do non-charismatic Christians hold so closely to what the Bible teaches, and place so little importance upon human experience and understanding? Simply because "faith cometh by hearing, and hearing by the word of God" (Romans 10:17). Scripture does not teach us that faith comes through a dramatic, emotional experience. The Holy Spirit led Paul to tell us that the *gospel* is the power of God unto salvation (Romans 1:16). Paul plainly tells us in II Timothy 3:16 that all *Scripture* is God-breathed and profitable for our doctrine, instruction, rebuke, and correction.

God emphasizes in both the Old and New Testaments that His Word is the only legitimate authority for establishing what we should believe. Isaiah declares, "If they speak not according to this word, it is because there is no light in them" (Isaiah 8:20). And the Apostle John gave a severe warning that "if any man shall add unto these things, God shall add unto him the plagues that are written in this book: And if any man shall take away from the words of the book of this prophecy, God shall take away his part out of the book of life, and out of the holy city, and from the things which are written in this book" (Revelation 22:19).

Certainly no one can deny that God considers tampering with His Word in any way a great offense. And I'm sure that when the charismatics make such claims, as did Oral Roberts, that the Holy Spirit acts sovereignly in exception to His Word in some cases of tongues-speaking, God does not gloss it over or consider it a minor thing. The Bible is God's complete written revelation to man, and He makes no provision for further revelation, even the Holy Spirit's alleged "sovereign actions."

The Scripture was complete when John laid down his pen after writing the book of the Revelation, and God will not reveal anything more to man in the way of visions, audible speech, dreams, or by any other supernatural means. Only when time is ended will we "know also as [we are] known" (I Corinthians 13:12). Until then, God's Word is our *sole authority* for all matters of faith and practice.

Just Suppose...

Let us look in on a charismatic meeting and note that three people have already spoken in tongues in turn, with interpreters. Let us now assume for a moment that these three people claim to have spoken in the power of the Holy Spirit and under His control. But as we listen, here is another who gives a message in tongues, followed by interpretation. As a matter of fact, before the meeting is concluded, there are several more. Knowing beyond the possibility of doubt that God the Holy Spirit will not perform in any way inconsistent with His Word, we realize that the fourth speaker and all of those following are not acting in the power of the Holy Spirit. This is a fact that cannot be denied if we accept the authority of the Word of God. And since those speaking in tongues are not speaking in the power of the Holy Spirit then it is obvious that neither are those who are interpreting doing so in His power. What then must we conclude?

What Spirit?

This brings us to a very significant question. Since these messages in strange tongues violate Biblical guidelines and are obviously not from the Holy Spirit, what spirit *are* they from? We could conclude that both the speaking with a tongue and the interpretation of it were expressions of man's emotional nature and that they came from his own spirit. But then we have to ask the question, "Is it possible for man strictly in his own spirit to speak in this manner?" Here we have people making strange ecstatic sounds and supposedly using some supernatural tongue, while others are manufacturing some kind of an interpretation. All of them are deliberately violating the Word of God and are posing as ministers in the power of and under the control of the Holy Spirit. I think we must conclude at this point that we have here more than mere expressions of man's emotional nature coming solely from his own spirit. We are forced to believe that these messages do not come from the Holy Spirit. It is my opinion that they derive from an evil spirit, for Satan and his followers have made a career of violating God's Word.

If I am correct in thinking that these messages had to come from an evil spirit, what does it say about the source of the messages of the first three speakers which were similar to these messages? Are the first messages valid? No one in the congregation, including the pastor, seemed to notice any difference, and the people seemed to be equally "blessed" by the false interpretations as by the first three. Therefore, I conclude in the light of the totality of Scripture that the first tongues, too, were not of the Holy Spirit, but derived from an evil spirit.

Satanic Origin

Dr. J. Vernon McGee writes in *Talking in Tongues* that speaking in tongues might be explained on a psychological basis involving auto-suggestion or self-hypnosis. He offers: "Now let me mention the second possible explanation. Tongues can be Satanic, and for this reason the believer should be very careful of them. Now I am not saying that all folk who talk in tongues are demon-possessed. Certainly not! But there are many cases on record both from heathen and Christian sources that prove that Satan can produce the phenomenon of speaking in tongues. We need to watch the Word of God in this connection. I'll tell you why. Our Lord said, 'For there shall arise false Christs, and false prophets, and shall shew great signs and wonders; insomuch that, if it were possible, they shall deceive the very elect' (Matthew 24:24)." He then quotes Revelation 13:13,14, which tells of the great wonders that will be performed by the false prophet during the Tribulation, and of the speaking by the image of the Beast predicted in Revelation 13:15. Dr. McGee feels the image's speech will include every human language, and that these languages will be the direct result of the working of Satan.

Could not Satan be producing tongues-speaking today to draw people's attention from the written word of God in order to elevate an emotional experience as the authority for determining one's beliefs and fellowship?

Mediumistic in Nature

In his book, *The Strife of Tongues*, Dr. Kurt Koch draws some interesting conclusions about speaking in tongues. He has found that people of all religions, races, nations, cultures, and intellectual levels speak in tongues. Many of these have been spiritist mediums speaking in strange languages while in a demonic trance. One medium in particular spoke 25 distinct languages, none of which he could ordinarily speak. Dr. Koch says this proves that not all speaking in tongues is a gift of the Holy Spirit. However, it *is* usually found in conjunction with highly emotional and excitable conditions, which can be caused by a variety of things including alcohol, drugs, dancing, and hypnotic suggestion.

Dr. Koch goes on to point out that those areas of the world which are seeing immense growth in satanic activity are also experiencing rapid growth in the tongues movement. He attributes this to the fact that people who have mediumistic tendencies are quicker to respond to speaking in tongues than are others. Many times people do not realize that they are mediumistic, and others discover their mediumism only by chance, but mediumistically-inclined people comprise about 8-10 percent of the Western world and 90 percent or more of the Eastern world.

Dr. Koch concludes that since so many people are mediumistic, some of them who become Christians carry this latent mediumism over into their new lives. When they later discover that they can speak in tongues, they believe that they have been given this ability by the Holy Spirit. Actually, it is only an outgrowth of their mediumistic powers. It is in no way related to the Holy Spirit, for He does not use such powers (Acts 16:16-18).

Because of the widespread mediumism in the world, even among Christians, we need to ask ourselves, "Are the tongues-speakers really manifesting the power of the Holy Spirit, or is this a demonic manifestation?" The Christian needs to be ever aware of the possible danger involved in this questionable practice, and to allow the Holy Spirit to control his life.

Chapter 8

Talk about Confusion!

And now, concluding our warning that the charismatic emphasis may really involve a relationship with the spirit of Satan rather than the Spirit of God, I want to call your attention to an incident which is recorded by Dr. James D. Bales, in his book *Pat Boone and The Gift of Tongues*. Beginning on page 232, under the heading "Human Jesus?" he reports: "Dean and Joyce Dennis were among the first converts whom Pat Boone helped make to Pentecostalism. In a Pentecostal journal, whose editor thinks he is led by the Spirit to publish testimonies, Joyce Dennis tells some things about her conversion. For nine or ten years she had felt, most of the time, that '*something* was wrong....' Finally, 'I gave up. Very little really mattered to me, anymore.'

" 'With nowhere else to turn, I cried out to God, someone I didn't really know. I remembered a warm Jesus who had come to me years before in a novel I read, *The Last Temptation of Christ. That* was the Jesus I wanted—the real, human One; the One that would just hold me and love me just as I was. Into His arms I went, and said, "Teach me, Lord!" His plan for my life since that time has been quite painful, but growth *is* painful!' (*Testimony*, No. 31, 1970, p. 10.) We can sympathize with her despair, but this reference to 'a warm Jesus who had come to me years before in a novel I read...' sickens the author and discredits her guidance system and that of the editor who would print such a statement. Although Joyce Dennis refused to give a friend the name of the author of the novel, when the author phoned her and asked if this was the novel by Nikos Kazantzakis, she said that it was.

"*Who was Kazantzakis?* He was a Cretan whose lies are well described by an ancient Cretan prophet: 'Cretans are always liars... This testimony is true.' (Titus 1:12-13.) Out of the dark depravity of his reprobate mind, which refused to retain and honor God in his knowledge (Romans 1:28), he created a Jesus. Of him we say, 'yea, let God be found true, but every man a liar...' (Romans 3:4) His teachers, whom he followed at different times, were Homer, Nietzsche, Bergson, Buddha, and Lenin (*Saturday Review*, Oct. 14, 1967, p. 51). Then, it seems, he became his own disciple. Out of the depth of his arrogance and pride this blasphemous sinner decided to create a new Christ. 'Thus at the age of fifty, he threw all his energies into what he considered his sole duty—to forge, like Joyce, the uncreated conscience of his race; to become a priest of the imagination.

" 'He was not primarily interested in reinterpreting Christ or in disagreeing with, or reforming, the Church. He wanted, rather, to lift Christ out of the Church altogether, and— since in the twentieth century the old era was dead or dying—to rise to the occasion and exercise man's right (and duty) to fashion a new saviour and thereby rescue himself from a moral and spiritual void.' (*The Last Temptation of Christ*, New York: Bantam Books, 1968, pp. 491, 495-496).

"*What kind of Jesus did Kazantzakis create in his novel?* His Jesus is not our Jesus, so we shall label his the K-Jesus, or K-J. *First*, K-J beat himself with a 'strap studded with two rows of sharp nails. . .' On one occasion he scourged himself until the 'blood spurted out and splashed him' (13,79). *Second*, K-J said: 'It's my fault that Magdelene [sic] descended to prostitution; it's my fault that Israel still groans under the yoke . . .' (14). *Third*, someone came to K-J one night, but he did not know whether it was God or the devil. 'Who can tell them apart?' (15). *Fourth*, at his mother's bidding K-J went to Cana to choose a wife. He saw Magdalene: ' "It's her I want, her I want!" he cried, and he held out his hand to give her the rose. But as he did so, ten claws nailed themselves into his head and two

Talk about Confusion!/ 81

frenzied wings beat above him, tightly covering his temples. He shrieked and fell down on his face, frothing at the mouth. His unfortunate mother, writhing with shame, had to throw her kerchief over his head, lift him up in her arms and depart.' (25) *Fifth*, after a perverse dream under a tree, K-J said to the tree: ' "Farewell, my sister," he murmured. "Last night under your shelter I brought shame upon myself. Forgive me"!' (79). *Sixth*, K-J told Magdalene the whore, at her place of prostitution, that he had many sins; he begged her for forgiveness, and was going to the desert to expiate his sins (80-88). *Seventh*, K-J opened the door to the five foolish virgins, but Jesus Christ left it shut in the parable (210-211; Matthew 25:12-13). *Eighth*, K-J dreamed he was suckling with the lion cubs, his mother appeared in the dream, screamed, and woke him up. K-J then said to his sleeping mother: ' "Why did you wake me up?" he shouted at her. "I was with my brothers and my mother"!' (240). *Ninth*, K-J committed adultery with Magdalene and said their son would be called 'Paraclete, the Comforter!' (440-442). *Tenth*, K-J insanely thought on the cross that he had wives and children, and then realized he was on the cross and that he had not succumbed to the temptation to marry and have children (473-487).

"How can these things be? Joyce Dennis thinks she is miraculously guarded each day, and that she has at least some direct guidance (*Testimony*, 10-11). First, why, then, would

she speak of a 'warm Jesus who had come to me years before *in a novel I read* (italics by J.D.B.), *The Last Temptation of Christ. That* was the Jesus I wanted—the real, human One; the One that would just hold me and love me just as I was.' *Second*, when the author talked with her on the phone on July 25, 1970, she said the novel showed her the humanity of Jesus. The author replied: 'Kazantzakis' Jesus is not our Jesus.' We learn of the humanity of Jesus Christ from the New Testament, and not from a blasphemous creation of a reprobate mind. *Third*, Joyce wrote these things *after* she was supposedly baptized in the Holy Spirit. The editor of *Testimony* printed her statement, and he, supposedly, adapts and condenses testimonies as he is led by the Spirit. This case demonstrates that neither he nor Joyce Dennis have any miraculous guidance of the Spirit. If they did, surely the Spirit would have at least warned them against including the reference to the 'warm Jesus' in Kazantzakis' novel, and her statement '*That* was the Jesus I wanted . . .'

"How does the author explain such a reference? The author does not know the explanation, but he does know it is a demonstration that she does not have the guidance which she thinks she has. The author does not know how she explains it to herself. He told her he planned to write an article on this reference. In her letter of July 26, and obviously before she had seen the article for it was not then completed, she said: 'I can only give glory to God that he has counted me worthy to bear this reproach for his name, knowing that through it he will be glorified. I also claim the many blessings that will come to me as a result of what you do.' How can a horrible blunder like this be called the bearing of reproach for the name of God? She can get a blessing out of this, if it helps her to re-think and to abandon Pentecostalism. She also wrote: 'I will look forward to reading your description of God's work in my life.' Obviously, this incident has nothing to do with God's work in her life, but deals with her own terrible blunder."

Let's get back now to our consideration of the text of I Corinthians 14. In verses 29-32, Paul gives further instructions about the conduct of meetings in the local assemblies.

God Not Author of Confusion

Paul reminds us in verse 33 that "God is not the author of confusion, but of peace, as in all churches of the saints." The word "confusion" is a very strong one in the original language, meaning *instability, state of disturbance, anarchy*. In James 3:15 we learn that it is the result of "earthly, sensual, devilish" wisdom. James further tells us, "where envying and strife is, there is confusion and every evil work" (verse 16). Evidence of confusion and strife caused by the charismatic movement of our times is available in abundance. Families, churches, associations of churches and even entire denominations have felt and are feeling the divisive effect of this unscriptural movement.

Speaking of confusion, has there ever been a time when there was so much confusion among Christian people? Has there ever been a time when we have witnessed such an unholy mixture of the world and the church, contradicting doctrines, belief and unbelief? Today all are walking together under the amazingly broad banner of the charismatics.

One charismatic preacher states, "I know a minister who is so liberal he neither believes in the virgin birth or the resurrection. Yet he has recently received the baptism in the Spirit and exhibits a marvelous power in his ministry." A thinking Christian will realize that if this liberal indeed has power, it is not from God!

The Bible tells us not to be unequally yoked with unbelievers, but there are many such people in the ranks of the charismatics. Protestants who believe and teach the doctrine of baptismal regeneration, accept every manner of liberal doctrine, and support enthusiastically the National and World Councils of Churches, are welcome—even proudly promoted—in the charismatic ranks.

Roman Catholics, who believe and practice false doctrines, are very big in the ranks of the charismatics. In spite of their false teachings, they claim to have received "the blessing" or "the baptism" and they speak in tongues. If we are to believe these people, the Reformation was all for nothing because all that seems to be necessary for acceptance in these so-called evangelical and charismatic circles, doctrine or no doctrine, is to speak in tongues.

Dr. David J. duPlessis, a noted Pentecostal leader and director of Melodyland School of Theology, has recently said the Catholic charismatic renewal is proof that "the Roman Catholic Church is being shaken to its traditional foundations since Vatican II." He attributes the following statement of Pope John XXIII to the moving of God: "THE CHURCH NEEDS RENEWAL, and for this RENEWAL there must come a NEW PENTECOST, to bring the Church back to the image of the Book of Acts." duPlessis commented: "The only Ecumenism that I accept is that of the Holy Spirit, who moves upon all flesh. . . ."

It is quite obvious that Dr. duPlessis feels, as do most charismatics, that all that is needed for someone to be included in the charismatic movement is "Spirit baptism"—speaking in tongues. He does not mention the fact that people need to be born again, that they should live separated lives, or that they should be Spirit-filled according to the teaching of Ephesians 5. He simply says that the Holy Spirit moves upon all flesh (the charismatic explanation for speaking in tongues) and unites everyone in one big ecumenical body.

In the February 28, 1975 issue of *Christianity Today*, J. Rodman Williams writes this about charismatic fellowship: "Herein is ecumenicity of a profound kind in which there is a rediscovery of the original wellsprings of the life of the Church.... The charismatic movement has, I believe, been well described by Dr. John Mackay [an extreme liberal] as 'the chief hope of the ecumenical tomorrow.'" In other words, the charismatics believe they are the ones who will bring about the realization of the ungodly dream of a one-world church. They disregard doctrinal problems and matters of heresy as long as one speaks in tongues.

We must not overlook the confusion which is promoted through the use of Hollywood and TV entertainment figures. While remaining in the entertainment world and promoting the causes of that world, they are promoted as "Spirit-baptized Christians." People like Pat Boone, Dale Evans, and others appear in the night spots of Las Vegas and other places and then, perhaps on the following evening, entertain in some Christian youth rally or church meeting. When these performers are thus promoted, our Christian people are really being told that being filled with the Spirit doesn't preclude limitless participation and involvement in the things of the world. Is it any wonder that our young people in particular are so mixed up?

Seek Earnestly to Prophesy

That brings us to the last two verses of the chapter. In verse 39, Paul says, "Covet to prophesy." The word for "covet" in the original really means *desire, seek with zeal, pursue actively*. This is the same word used at the very beginning of the chapter. The Corinthians were to seek earnestly and continuously to prophesy. The urging of the apostle is that they should put all of their zeal into telling forth the grace and the glory of God's revelation.

Concerning the admonition to "forbid not to speak with tongues," Zodhiates points out, "Observe that the command to prophesy is connected with the command 'forbid not to speak with tongues,' not by an adversitive ('but') but by the connective 'and.' 'Tongues' here does not stand in contrast to prophesying but is regarded as a means of accomplishing it. To prophesy, you must make the counsels of God clear to your listeners. Unknown tongues cannot accomplish this. We have seen right along that Paul has used the singular form, 'a tongue,' with a singular subject, to refer to unknown ecstatic utterances, and the plural form, 'tongues,' with a singular subject, to refer to known, understandable languages. Tongues (understandable foreign languages) are consistent with the use of prophesy and are to be permitted. Such would not be the case if Paul were merely tolerating tongues speaking as opposed to prophecy. In the latter case, he would have said, 'Covet to prophesy, but forbid not to speak with a tongue if an interpreter is present.' But in this verse he makes no mention of an interpreter, which would seem to rule out ecstatic utterances. Why should he say, 'Forbid not to speak in ecstatic utterances such as lead unbelievers to think you mad when you practice them in public'?

"When necessary to accomplish the purpose of prophesying, you may speak in a foreign language, either by direct enablement of God or through having learned it naturally. Here, again, this is only acceptable where your hearers can understand you. Paul's whole thesis in this discussion on speaking in the public worship service is that whatever is said, whether in human languages or an unknown tongue, must be understandable, either directly or through an interpreter, if it is to edify the church. When telling the Corinthians not to forbid speaking in tongues, he must mean what he has already argued as being acceptable in the public worship service. The word 'tongues' in verse 39, is all inclusive, with the very basic assumption that 'tongues' are understood, whether they be an unknown tongue through an interpreter or any human language (the latter either directly understood by the hearers or interpreted through a translator).

"Paul may also have been afraid lest the Corinthians go to the other extreme and forbid speaking in foreign languages altogether. But these are deemed acceptable since they are interpretable."

Let All Things Be Done Decently and in Order

Paul then gives his final instructions concerning speaking with tongues, "Let all things be done decently and in order" (verse 40).

In his book *Charismatic Confusion*, Paul R. Van Gorder concludes, "This least spiritual of the churches, Corinth, had given a new weight to speaking with tongues. The confusion and disorder in their gatherings was indicative that this emphasis was not from God. Violation of these regulations in the Apostolic assembly marked the practiced gift as spurious. Christian people today who fail to observe these instructions, and yet contend that they have the gift of tongues, are being deceived."

Chapter 9

Practical Insights

*H*aving completed our investigation regarding the teaching of the Word of God about tongues let me set before you a number of other significant observations that are pertinent to our subject.

Great Men of God

I have read Christian history and have studied the lives of great men of God for many years. But I have never found a single instance where a mighty hero of the faith spoke in "unknown tongues." Theologians, missionaries, preachers, translators, earth-shaking evangelists—all have come under careful examination, and many have given testimony to the fullness of the Holy Spirit, but none has ever indicated that he spoke with tongues.

One of the church fathers, John Chrysostom, sometimes referred to as John the Golden Mouth, was one of the most eloquent preachers of all time and one of the best Bible commentators. As pastor of the fourth-century churches at Antioch and Constantinople, he expressed surprise at Paul's account of the tongues-speaking at Corinth. He felt that "the whole passage [I Corinthians 14] is exceedingly obscure and the obscurity is occasioned by our ignorance of the fact and the cessation of happenings which were common in those days but unexampled in our own."

Richard Trench, one of the clearest and most faithful theologians of the last century and author of *Notes of the Miracles of Our Lord*, wrote, "If the gift of tongues still survives among us, then it no longer does so under the same name nor with the same frequency and intensity as of old."

Some of the great evangelists have spoken very forcefully in opposition to the tongues movement. Dr. R. A. Torrey remarked that "the gift of tongues was so evidently abused in the early church, even as it is today, that it became necessary to warn people about it. God in His wisdom and love may well have considered it necessary to hold back this gift for a period of time. And we have no reason to presume that He has renewed the gift in our time, for it is quite certain that today's so-called tongues movement is not of God."

Doesn't it seem to you that if this movement were really of God and were profitable for the edification of the believers and glorification of the Lord, the great preachers would see this fact? Surely the Lord isn't allowing all these men to remain ignorant, or permitting them to miss out on a great blessing. It is only logical to conclude that the tongues movement is Scripturally unfounded, and is not necessary in the church today.

Tongues Not Stressed in New Testament

Let us once again notice that the phenomenon of tongues-speaking is not seen in the life and experience of our Lord Jesus. In many New Testament passages we are told that He was filled with the Holy Spirit. He was our best example of the blessed gifts of the Spirit, but *He never spoke in tongues.*

Once again I remind you that tongues is not referred to anywhere in the Gospels, nor in the lists of spiritual gifts recorded in Romans 12:4-8 and Ephesians 4:11. Tongues is not referred to in any of the Epistles of Paul except I Corinthians. Not even in Paul's second letter to the Corinthian church is tongues mentioned. It is not mentioned in the Pastoral Epistles (I, II Timothy, Titus). It is not mentioned in the book of Hebrews. It is not mentioned in the General Epistles (James, I, II Peter, I, II, III John, Jude). And it is not mentioned in the book of Revelation. With such a lack of emphasis shown in the Scriptures, ask yourself—Is it really right to make tongues important?

What About the Churches?

You may say that the early churches were deeply involved in the use of tongues. But look again. With the exception of Corinth, tongues-speaking is never seen in any of the New Testament churches—it is not in the churches of Macedonia, Achaia, Judaea, Samaria, Asia, Rome, or any other place. It is seen only in the church at Corinth, a congregation that Paul referred to as "carnal," a people whom Paul described as "babes in Christ." Obviously, then, the gift of tongues was *not* prominent in the early churches as some of the modern advocates of tongues-speaking would have us believe. And the one church it was seen in was by no means exemplary.

Not Essential

Why do the charismatics feel tongues is so important in the life of a believer? The gift is not mentioned as a part of the fruit of the Spirit in Galatians 5, or anywhere else in the Bible. It is not listed among the qualifications for deacons or elders, nor is it given as a mark of spiritual maturity. In fact, tongues is not given as a prerequisite for anything, nor is the gift even encouraged anywhere in Scripture. It seems to me that the charismatics have an acute case of majoring on the minors. We need to take care to base our idea of spirituality on the Word of God, not on emotional excitement, or perhaps even demonic control.

Practice Makes Perfect?

Anyone reading or hearing the instructions that are frequently given by charismatics to those who want to know how to receive the gift of tongues should be able to recognize how ridiculous the whole matter is. For example, one tongues-speaking leader gave these directions: "Raise up your hands and your eyes to Heaven and begin speaking words, sounds, syllables, and keep it up, faster, faster, faster, louder, words, more words, faster, faster, and it has happened! You have received the baptism of the Holy Ghost!" Sometimes those who are seeking this gift are encouraged to remain in "tarrying meetings." In these they are taught to imitate the leader in saying "ah-bah, ah-bah, beta," while the leader shakes the seeker's lower jaw to loosen it so the gift will come.

Do you really think the Holy Spirit—the moving, mighty Spirit of God—is thus controlled and directed by loosening the jaw or by gibberish or senseless sounds? Nowhere in Scripture is there even a suggestion of such practices in connection with legitimate tongues-speaking. Therefore we must conclude that these practices are unscriptural and have no rightful place in the life of the believer.

Tragically Divisive!

Because of the problems in the charismatic movement the Union Baptist Association of the Southern Baptist Convention (Houston, Texas) has adopted a resolution condemning the movement as unscriptural and being of the devil. The resolution said every church should be on guard against efforts of the devil to infiltrate the fellowship with false doctrines and divisive influences. This action followed motions by the Dallas Baptist Association to remove charismatic churches from its fellowship after a year of controversy over neo-pentecostal activities in some churches. The Trenton Baptist Association in Louisiana has ousted a church with charismatic ministry. The Cincinnati, Ohio, Baptist Association earlier removed two churches with charismatic ministries from its fellowship. Later the Dallas Baptist Association, the largest group in the Southern Baptist Convention, ousted two member churches that openly practiced tongues and alleged "faith healing." Certainly all these groups are not just "beating a dead horse." Their concern is justified.

Sadly enough the tongues-speakers are unteachable. Their superior attitude causes them to evaluate all teaching according to what they believe, and consequently their minds are closed to the ideas of others.

Ephesians 4:3 admonishes us to strive for unity in the Spirit, but these supposedly Spirit-controlled people have a tendency to split churches. They oppose those in the body with differing opinions, and side with others of their kind. No wonder churches are splitting faster than we can count them!

When these quarrelsome people have caused sufficient problems in one church, they hop to another. And they don't mind it if they succeed in pulling some people with them. They do not develop a faithfulness to a local body, and they see nothing wrong with sharply criticizing the members of a church. This behavior certainly does not exemplify the Holy Spirit's control that they claim to manifest.

Finally, I quote the words of Dr. Gerald I. Gerig, which he addressed to a large Baptist congregation in California. He was interim pastor at the time, and was urging the congregation to pray for clear direction for the pulpit committee. Dr. Gerig explained:

"We want our church to be doctrinally sound for the new pastor. The past days have been days when we have taken our stand regarding the teaching on the Holy Spirit. We know that there are many who do not agree with our position, but we must be true to what we believe the Word of God teaches, and then practice this in love. . . . 'We believe that the so-called "speaking in tongues" (ecstatic utterances) is not to be practiced by any member of this church in public or private, on the authority of God's Word.' "

To the conclusions of this church I say a hearty "Amen!" Any matter as divisive and problematic as tongues has no place in the body of Christ. Instead we need sincere and cooperative efforts to unify believers through a thorough study of the Word and heartfelt prayer. May we always strive to weed out those things that will antagonize and divide Christian brothers, and seek to "keep unity of the Spirit in the bond of peace" (Ephesians 4:3).

Chapter 10

Tongues and the "Baptism"

One of the basic disagreements I have with charismatics centers on the meaning of "the baptism of the Holy Spirit." David duPlessis, an influential figure in the charismatic movement, links tongues-speaking with what he calls "baptism in the spirit." He claims that speaking in tongues should be considered the simple consequence of the baptism in the Spirit. He views the Holy Spirit as the gift and tongues as the result.

Since charismatics are so insistent on relating the baptism of the Holy Spirit with tongues, we need to study what the Bible says about the baptism.

Always Related to the Church

Before we get down to the specifics of Spirit baptism, it is important to keep in mind that the baptism is always related to the church. In John 14:16 Jesus told His disciples He would "pray the Father, and he shall give you [who will constitute the church] another Comforter, that he may abide with you forever." Christ was going to leave earth. He had ministered wonderfully and constantly while here, but now He was leaving and the disciples would not have Him to help them, to be their Comforter. However, He promised to send another Comforter, who would take His place and abide with them forever. But just who was that Comforter going to be? The Lord graciously answered that question—"Even the Spirit of truth; whom the world cannot receive, because it seeth him not, neither knoweth him: but ye know him; for he dwelleth with you, and shall be in you" (verse 17).

In Old Testament times and until the fulfillment of Christ's promise, the Holy Spirit dwelled *with* the saints. But Jesus said there would come a time when that would be changed and for the first time in the history of mankind the Holy Spirit would be *in* people. The old economy was passing into the background and Jesus Christ was about to institute a new arrangement, a new program and a new dwelling place for the Spirit of God—the hearts and lives of God's people.

Amazing, but True

In verse 20 we read, "At that day [when the Comforter comes] ye shall know that I am in my Father, and ye in me, and I in you." A short verse, to be sure, but it is nonetheless significant. We see in this verse the unity of the Son and the Father. They cannot be separated, for they are one. We next see the oneness of the believer with the Saviour. When the Spirit of God applies the cleansing blood to the heart of a sinner and regenerates him, by God's grace Christ enters into him.

Not only is Christ in us, but we are in Him. At the point of salvation we become part of the body of Christ. How is this brought about? By the baptism of the Holy Spirit.

Let's Find Out

What does the Bible say about Spirit baptism? There are only seven passages in the New Testament pertaining to the subject. The first of these is in Matthew 3:11, and is repeated in Mark 1:8; Luke 3:16; and John 1:33. In these passages John the Baptist is prophesying about Christ's coming. He makes it clear that the baptizing will be performed by Christ and will be with the "Holy Ghost, and with fire." The fifth reference to Spirit baptism is in Acts 1:5. Jesus here repeats John's statement, but adds that the baptism will take place "not many days hence."

So far all the passages have been based on John the Baptist's words, and all are predictive. They tell that there was an event coming when the Lord Jesus would do something that He had never done before—something new, something special, something dramatic, something climactic. What would it be? The baptism with the Holy Spirit and with fire!

The Fulfillment

When did it happen? When were these predictions fulfilled? Look at the sixth reference, Acts 11:16, where Peter is speaking. "Then remembered [past tense] I the word of the Lord, how that he said, John indeed baptized with water; but ye shall be baptized with the Holy Ghost." Peter is recounting the day when he spoke to the Gentiles in the household of Cornelius. Suddenly the Spirit of God had fallen "on all them which heard the word" in tremendous power, and they received the Holy Ghost in His fullness and began to speak with other languages (Acts 10:44-46). When this happened Peter immediately remembered what John had said, and recognized this as a fulfillment of John's prophecy. In Acts 11:17 he further suggests that for the Jews, the day of Pentecost was the fulfillment of John's promise, although the word "baptism" is not used in the Acts 2 narrative.

People often make the mistake of equating the amazing performance of the 120 who were gathered together in the Upper Room at Pentecost with Spirit baptism. On the day of Pentecost two distinct things happened—first, there was the baptism of the Holy Spirit and second, there was the infilling. When the 120 left the Upper Room and went out into the streets of the city witnessing to everyone in sight, it was not a direct result of the baptism but of the Spirit's filling. Later, we'll study the Spirit's filling in close detail, but for now we'll concentrate on the distinction between

Spirit baptism and Spirit filling.

Something New

That brings us to the final reference to Spirit baptism—I Corinthians 12:13. It is here that we learn about the development of the body of Jesus Christ. "For as the body is one, and hath many members, and all the members of that one body, being many, are one body: so also is Christ" (verse 12).

Perhaps we have never looked at Christ that way before. We have thought about Him as an individual, but here we are taught that the body of Christ is composed also of all who believe in Him. As the human body is one, "so also is Christ." The human body has arms, legs, ears, a nose, a mouth, a tongue, hair and innumerable other members, but still is one body. So it is with Christ—He has many members, yet all the members are one with Him.

You may be wondering, "How do we get into the body?" The answer is in verse 13 where we read, "For by one Spirit are we all baptized into one body, whether we be Jews or Gentiles, whether we be bond or free; and have been all made to drink into one Spirit." We notice that the baptizer here is the Holy Spirit. He was sent to minister to believers, and an integral part of that ministry is taking the regenerated sinner and placing him into the body of Christ—by His baptism.

The passage is quite specific in telling us that *every* redeemed sinner—without any distinction—is placed into the body of the Lord Jesus Christ! Whether you are a perfect Christian or a blatantly imperfect one, you are in the body of Christ. Though you may slip and fall and fail, you are in the body, and will remain there forever.

Why Seek It?

Since every child of God is guaranteed a place in the body of Christ through the baptism of the Holy Spirit, why is it that the charismatics so dogmatically insist we are to seek the baptism? Does it not seem strange to you that these people spend so much time and effort coaxing the baptism along, when in reality they have already been baptized if they are born again? Nowhere in Scripture are we told to seek the baptism of the Holy Spirit. In fact, I Corinthians 12:13 makes it extremely clear that it is a waste of time to seek the baptism.

Some of the charismatics bring up the argument that when Paul said "we all" he didn't mean all born-again believers, but all spiritual believers. I would like to point out that this letter was to the most carnal church the apostle ministered to. Certainly he would not be so foolish as to say "we" and include the Corinthians if spirituality were a requirement for the baptism, because the Corinthians were far from spiritual.

No, the only thing necessary for someone to receive the baptism of the Holy Spirit is faith in Christ. At the moment we exercise that faith, we are baptized into His body. Why should we seek a false tongues-related "baptism"? Our sufficiency is in Christ, and we are in Christ from the moment of our salvation—without tongues-speaking.

Chapter 11

Be Filled with the Spirit

*B*ecause non-charismatic believers do not seek the baptism of the Spirit and the experience of speaking in tongues, charismatics often conclude that non-charismatic believers are not interested in the Spirit's power. Not so. Believers who rest their case on Scripture, not on experience, want to live daily with the kind of effectiveness the Bible promises to all who honor the God of the Bible.

What does the Bible say about the way to lead an effective Christian life? Does it tell us to find someone we respect and copy whatever religious experience he cites as the greatest thing that ever happened to him? Indeed, it does not, for our experience must be based on doctrine. Our doctrine must not be based on experience.

So let's view the effective, divinely blessed life from the perspective of Scripture.

Your Walk, Not Your Talk

In Ephesians Paul writes to inform the church at Ephesus about the blessings which all Christians have in Christ (Ephesians 1:3). He points out that we have forgiveness of sins (verse 7), a tremendous inheritance (verse 11), security (verses 13,14), enlightenment (verse 18), eternal life (2:1), God's workmanship in our lives (verse 10), heavenly citizenship (verse 19), access to God (3:12), immeasurable divine love (verse 19), and the promise of power (verse 20). All of this takes up three chapters—a rather lengthy basis for the implications Paul presents in chapters 4—6 of his epistle.

In chapters 4—6 the apostle shifts from the mainly doctrinal section of Ephesians to the mainly experiential. In other words, he moves from the area of doctrine into the area of duty. And this is fitting, for right behavior, as I have already suggested, must follow right believing. An understanding of what we have *in Christ* results in a proper demonstration of what Christ is doing *in us*. In chapters 4—6 Paul talks about living for Christ on a daily basis. He explains in chapter 4 that people ought to see a difference in us since we have come to know Christ as our personal Saviour. In chapter 5 his emphasis is on being Christ-like "in church" (verses 19,20) and in the marital relationship (verses 22-33). In chapter 6 he continues this emphasis to include Christ-likeness in the parent-child relationship and in the employer-employee relationship as well. Then he explains that there is a fight involved in living for Christ, for the devil throws his heavy artillery at all who desire to honor Christ (verses 10-18).

The fact is, then, the effective Christian life shows up in what we are inside and what we are at church, at home, on the job—anywhere and everywhere. This is why Ephesians may be referred to as a classic example of how doctrine and duty link together. It begins in the heavenlies and ends in the home.

Now, how can we be like Jesus in the home and in the throng? Ephesians 5:18 is the key that unlocks the mystery: "Be not drunk with wine, wherein is excess; but be filled with the Spirit." Let's look closely at Paul's inspired command.

Not Optional!

In the first place, observe that it is a command. Both negative and positive. On the negative side we are not to be influenced by wine. It must not be in control of us in any way. (Christians are wise to practice total abstinence as the safest protection against being under the influence of wine.) The positive command concerns our relationship to the Holy Spirit. Just as we are not to be influenced—controlled—by wine, we are commanded to be controlled by the Holy Spirit.

The word "filled" in Ephesians 5:18 carries the idea of control, for it is in the context of the influence wine can exert on a person. We often use "filled" in this way in our daily conversation. We talk about someone being filled with fear at the thought of boarding an airplane, being enclosed in close quarters, falling into water, looking down from the top of a high building, or coming face to face with a vicious dog. What do we mean? We mean the person in any of these situations was controlled by fear.

More Than Once

But how often should a Christian be controlled by the Holy Spirit? Just once? No, the idea of the command in Ephesians 5:18 is *Be being continually filled with the Spirit.* Paul knew full well that there is no such thing as instant holiness or instant victory in the Christian life. Living for the Lord is a daily battle, because we face a daily foe—Satan, according to Ephesians 6:11-16. We shall know either the daily control of the Holy Spirit over our thoughts and actions, or we shall experience daily defeat at the hands of the wicked one.

The big question, then, is, How shall we be continually being filled with the Holy Spirit?

Hands Off!

It seems to me that we must get our answer

from Scripture. Romans 12:1 indicates that God wants to control us and therefore commands us to offer our bodies as sacrifices to Him for the working out of His will. It is logical, then, that we must make ourselves available to God in order to possess the Spirit's power that is available to us. Certainly the Spirit will not grant His power for any kind of conduct that is foreign to God's will for us.

Have you, then, offered your body as a living sacrifice to God? As a Christian, bought with the blood of Christ, you really don't have any title deed to your own body and life. The Lord owns you and has the right to claim your body and life for the performance of His good, acceptable and perfect will.

The Heart of the Issue

Something else—fill your heart with Scripture. This is what Paul recommends in Colossians 3:16. And, interestingly, he suggests in this verse that the results of filling your heart with Scripture will be the same as the results he describes in Ephesians 5:19,20. You see the point, don't you? The Spirit always uses the Word to accomplish His purposes. He never violates the Word or bypasses it. He never elevates human experience above divine revelation.

If you want to be continually filled with the Spirit, develop a program of daily Bible reading. But be sure to obey what you read.

Some persons can have a head full of Bible verses and a heart full of sin. We must permit the Word to get through our minds to our hearts so that it changes what we are deep down inside. Then we shall become the illustrated Word in our daily relationships.

Quench Not!

The Scripture tells us, too, not to quench the Spirit (I Thessalonians 5:19). You see, the Holy Spirit wants to lead us daily to do what pleases God. So we ought to cooperate with Him. Rather than refusing to witness to the lost, refusing to pray, refusing to right a wrong, refusing to praise, we ought to do what the Spirit desires—witness, pray, perform deeds of kindness, praise, and a lot more.

Grieve Not!

Furthermore, the Bible exhorts us to "grieve not the holy Spirit of God" (Ephesians 4:30a). Since the Spirit is a Person, He may be grieved, and surely He is grieved when we fail to attach a top priority to pleasing God. When we participate in worldly activities, harbor evil thoughts and selfish ambitions, and neglect the Word, we are grieving the One who has come to shape us into the image of Christ and make us fruitful (II Corinthians 3:18; Galatians 5:22,23).

Put it all together. In order to enjoy the continual, day-by-day filling with God's Spirit, we must yield ourselves to God, study and obey the Word, and cooperate with the Holy Spirit as He endeavors to make us the kind of Christians we ought to be—powerful and Christ-like.

It Makes a Difference

Charismatics may be interested in knowing that some of the greatest Bible teachers and evangelists of all time were non-charismatic. They never sought the experience of tongues-speaking. Nor did they encourage others to speak in tongues. Yet they were powerful servants of God because they were compliant with the Scriptural commands to yield unreservedly to God, to walk in the light of the Word, and to cooperate with the Spirit's ministry of shaping them into Christ-like, productive believers. Charles Haddon Spurgeon, A. T. Pierson, and Dwight L. Moody are just a few choice servants of God who testified to the difference it made to their ministries to be filled with the Spirit.

And it does make a difference to be filled continually with the Holy Spirit. Paul points to one of the differences in Galatians 5:16-26. He explains that the Spirit-filled life is a "walk" in the Spirit, bringing cooperation and peace to the ranks of a local church's membership. Without the continual influence of the Spirit, there is bound to be rancor and divisiveness. Paul projects the same concept into the Ephesian church context by pointing out in Ephesians 5:19-21 that Spirit-filled Christians enjoy their fellowship together. Their joy is contagious, and their submissiveness obvious.

What happens when charismatics infiltrate a church? It isn't long before they parade a false spirituality, accuse others of being unspiritual because they haven't had the "experience," and discredit the pastor as someone who doesn't teach the "full" gospel. Such persons are anything but submissive and cooperative. They spread unhappiness, not joy. And they feed the flames of dissension instead of the fires of mutual love and devotion to God.

A word of caution, then, is in order. We must mark those who cause dissension and provide no opportunity for them to lead us astray. But a word of challenge is also in order. We ought to be so Spirit-filled that our lives will testify to the Spirit's power in using the Bible to make us victorious and appealing servants of Christ.

In his book *The Holy Spirit in Today's World*, W. A. Criswell gives us a helpful challenge. He suggests that the filling with the Spirit implies that the Spirit is to pervade our lives. He is to engulf us with His holy presence, His mighty power, and His blessed activity. Our whole self—heart, soul and life—is to be His possession. The result will be living that perpetually glorifies God.

Jesus, fill now with thy Spirit
Hearts that full surrender know;
That the streams of living water
From our inner man may flow.

Channels only, blessed Master,
But with all Thy wondrous power
Flowing through us, Thou canst use us
Every day and every hour.

Chapter 12

Why We Must Take a Stand

After identifying the gifts of the ascended Christ to His churches, Paul explains that the purpose of these gifts is "for the perfecting of the saints, for the work of the ministry, for the edifying of the body of Christ: Till we all come in the unity of the faith, and of the knowledge of the Son of God, unto a perfect man, unto the measure of the stature of the fulness of Christ" (Ephesians 4:7-13).

Next Paul stresses a matter of great importance, admonishing "that we henceforth be no more children, tossed to and fro, and carried about with every wind of doctrine, by the sleight of men, and cunning craftiness, whereby they lie in wait to deceive; But speaking the truth in love, may grow up into him in all things, which is the head, even Christ" (Ephesians 4:14,15).

Why We Must Take a Stand/ 119

The winds of strange doctrine are blowing today more than ever before. Multitudes of Bible-believing Christians are being "tossed to and fro, and carried about" because of teaching that is not honestly based upon the Word of God, but is taught by "cunning craftiness" and deception.

God does not want us to be like "a reed shaken with the wind" (Matthew 11:7). He wants us to stand solidly, stalwartly and strong. This is the only way we can be effective in contributing to the "increase of the body unto the edifying of itself" (Ephesians 4:16).

It is never easy to take a stand regarding controversial matters, and it will certainly not be easy for us to take a stand on this subject of tongues. Criticism will come. Accusations will follow. You will be told that you are negative when you should be positive. People will suggest that you are lacking in love. Those who are supremely divisive will go so far as to charge *you* with being divisive. They may even warn that you could be guilty of committing the unpardonable sin. But no matter how much criticism you receive, and no matter how much you are persecuted, you *must* take a stand on this matter of tongues.

Scripture's Example

In these days of such strong emphasis on "positive thinking," how are we to react when people accuse us of being negative? Shall we hang our heads and apologize for enunciating a Scriptural position? Should we determine to be more tolerant of this error and be conciliatory in our attitude?

D. Martin Lloyd-Jones suggests in his commentary on Romans that "Because of our sinful state it is essential that truth should be stated negatively as well as positively. If man had not sinned, it would have been enough to give him the truth positively, but because he has sinned that is never enough. So you will find in the Scriptures everywhere, in the teaching portions, that there are negatives as well as positives.... The negative helps to focus attention on the teaching; it helps to underline it; it helps to define it.... This modern generation of Christians does not like negatives. They say, 'All we want is the positive truth; you need not bother about those negatives.' But the very fact that they say that means that they need the negatives very badly. They are displaying their ignorance, they are in the position described by this Apostle [Paul] in his Epistle to the Ephesians. They are like 'children, tossed to and fro, and carried about by every wind of doctrine.' The Scriptures safeguard our position by emphasizing negatives as well as positives."

If you will carefully check the teaching of the New Testament you will discover that there are as many negative passages as there are positive. Although "positive" and "possibility" thinking has been greatly popularized in these modern days, the Bible is well-balanced between negative and positive. And you cannot teach the Bible and be really effective in your service for Christ unless your witness is equally balanced. Do not be afraid of being called negative, for the Bible is our authority, teaching us to have a balance between positive and negative.

The Truth Supreme

In order to avoid being "tossed to and fro, and carried about with every wind of doctrine" by men who seek, intentionally or otherwise, to deceive, we must be concerned about "speaking the truth." We cannot be "ever learning, and never able to come to the knowledge of the truth" (II Timothy 3:7). We need to know the truth and, at all costs, stand for it.

We can find out from Jesus that God's Word is truth (John 17:17), and we must make every decision on that basis. Regardless of emotional reactions or testimonies about experiences, our responsibility is to be faithful to the Word of God and to defend it at any cost. It is up to the Christian to "earnestly contend for the faith which was once delivered unto the saints" (Jude 3).

Sometimes a loved one, perhaps even a member of our own family, will get involved in doctrinal error. But the fact that we love that person and think highly of him or her doesn't lessen the seriousness of the error. We dare not compromise the truth. Indeed, our attitude must be to "let God be true, but every man a liar" (Romans 3:4).

In His Steps

Jesus dealt with sin and error. He constantly exposed the false teachers of His day and warned us that there would be many false teachers in the generations ahead. If we would follow Him, it is inevitable that we will sometimes find ourselves taking unpopular stands and being involved in matters of controversy.

In these crucial times, we should especially take to heart what Jesus said in Matthew 7:21-23: "Not every one that saith unto me, Lord, Lord, shall enter into the kingdom of heaven; but he that doeth the will of my father which is in heaven. Many will say to me in that day, Lord, Lord, have we not prophesied in thy name? and in thy name have cast out devils? and in thy name done many wonderful works? And then will I profess unto them, I never knew you: depart from me, ye that work iniquity."

Here Jesus warns us that there will be many who will come with a strong profession, testifying to great and tremendous experiences in His name. But our Saviour refers to their work as "iniquity," and declares unto them, "I never knew you." Since Jesus will expose these as false "workers of iniquity," it naturally follows that anyone coming to us with similar credentials should be scrutinized most carefully.

Notice that there will be *many* of these workers who will cast out demons, prophesy, and do other wonders *in the name of Jesus.* But it is not the profession; it is not the experiences; and it is not even the use of the name of Jesus that God is looking for. "He that doeth the will of my Father" is the one Christ acknowledges and calls His own. All others are rejected.

In Matthew 15 we hear Jesus saying "Ye made the commandment of God of none effect by your tradition." He calls the scribes and Pharisees "hypocrites" and says, "their heart is far from me. But in vain do they worship me, teaching for doctrines the commandments of men" (verses 6-9). He rebukes the Sadducees and blisters the Pharisees in Matthew 23:13-35, where we see such excoriating denunciation as cannot be found anywhere else in the Bible. Elsewhere He charges them with "making the Word of God of none effect" (Mark 7:13).

On one occasion it was even necessary for Jesus to rebuke Peter. "But he turned, and said unto Peter, Get thee behind me, Satan: thou art an offence unto me: for thou savorest not the things that be of God, but those that be of men" (Matthew 16:23).

The record is strong and clear: our Saviour was stedfast in His fight for the faith. If we would follow Jesus, we will not be afraid to take a clear and uncompromising stand for the truth and against every form of error.

The Apostle Paul

Although there are many Biblical examples of taking a strong stand against error, perhaps the most vocal example is the Apostle Paul.

He is the one who directs us to "preach the Word . . . reprove, rebuke, exhort with all longsuffering and doctrine" (II Timothy 4:2). In verse 7 of the same chapter he says, "I have fought a good fight, I have finished my course, I have kept the faith."

A part of his fighting the good fight and keeping the faith involved rebuking Peter. In Galatians 2 we see Paul's concern for the "truth of the gospel." He continues to tell how Peter gave way to compromise in order to please the brethren and to be one of the crowd, and declares that Peter was guilty of walking "not uprightly according to the truth of the gospel." As a result of this Paul "withstood [Peter] to the face, because he was to be blamed." He charged Peter with being hypocritical even to the point of affecting Barnabas, who "was carried away with their dissimulation" (verses 5-14).

Certainly no one can deny that Paul determinedly stood for what he knew to be right. Not even another of the apostles could cow him into being soft on doctrinal error. He was a defender of the truth, an example of being faithful to the Word. May we, like Paul, finish our course, having fought a good fight, and knowing we kept the faith against all of Satan's attempts to destroy it.

Oppose Division

Our charismatic friends will sometimes

accuse us of being divisive simply because we point out that their practice of tongues is unbiblical and embraces error. But the real problem, when it comes to divisiveness, is the determination of these people, on the basis of carefully calculated strategy, to move into Bible-believing churches for the purpose of disseminating their false doctrine and turning people away from the truth.

In this regard, I have had people call me to tell me they were determined that one day my church be taken over by people who accept the charismatic position. I personally know of too many churches that have been divided, split up, and in some cases taken over completely by the charismatics, to take such threats lightly. In Romans 16:17 we are warned to "mark them which cause divisions and offences contrary to the doctrine which ye have learned; and avoid them."

The unity of the faith is extremely important to our Lord. He reminds us to be of "one mind striving together for the faith of the gospel" (Philippians 1:27). Because we are obligated before God to protect the unity of the church and of the faith we must take an unqualified stand against every effort to divide the ranks and to introduce error.

Interpersonal Obligations

Without a doubt, multitudes have been led down the primrose path of serious error simply because knowledgeable pastors and lay people were not willing to take a clear stand in these matters. Because they were unwilling to offend those who taught error, they were guilty of offending those who needed the truth. In these days of much confusion people are desperately in need of direction on the basis of the authority of God's Word. Those of us who know the truth must declare it as it is without fear, favor or hesitance. We need to provide solid opposition to those who would lead our friends, neighbors, loved ones and fellow church members astray. To do otherwise is to be less than faithful to our trust.

A Lack of Love?

I now want to deal with what is probably the most prevalent criticism of all: "You are lacking in love."

In all honesty, I think we will have to acknowledge that far too often we have been sadly deficient in this area of love. We need to face up to our failures and our needs in this regard. We need to wholeheartedly love the Lord, His Word, and His church, and we need to reflect that love in all of our contacts with people—saints and sinners alike!

We are willing to acknowledge our need for much improvement in regard to our spiritual love life, and without question we need to pursue it with much determination. But it is not a lack of love that causes us to defend the truth and oppose those who propagate error. Undoubtedly, our charismatic friends would like to have the world believe that we are lacking in love. They would like to embarrass us into believing that. But do not be misled. A lack of love is not inherent in dealing frankly with error any more than it was when Jesus spoke plainly of the "workers of iniquity."

Incidentally, the "great lovers" of many compromising churches are not always as loving as they profess to be. Confront them with the truth, or expose their divisiveness, and you will soon discover that their love is not even skin deep.

One of the very best ways to demonstrate our love to both God and man is to expose error and throw the floodlight of truth upon the question involved. To stand by with closed lips when someone is expressing error or being exposed to error would reveal a total lack of love to God and His Word. It would also indicate sympathy for those who are responsible for the error. If we would really reflect our love for God, for His holy Word, and for others, we will hold forth the word of truth and raise high the standard of God's Word as a banner that cannot be ignored. We will insist with every bit of compassion we can command that "this is the way of the Lord." Allowing those around us to continue on in error without even attempting to correct them shows inconsideration on our part. "None of us liveth unto himself, and no man dieth unto himself" (Romans 14:7), so it is our responsibility to help others find the right way.

Above all, we must yield to the Word of God as the sole authority for every aspect of life. It is God's faultless message for us. We need no other message. With Scripture in our hearts we shall be able to discern truth from error and defeat the advances of Satan himself.